MW00681199

A Pocket Tour™ of Kidstuff on the Internet

Sara Armstrong, Ph.D.

San Francisco • Paris • Düsseldorf • Soest

SYBEX

Pocket Tour Concept:	Brenda Kienan
Acquisition and Development Editor:	Brenda Kienan
Editor:	Pat Coleman
Project Editors:	Malcolm Faulds, Laura Arendal
Technical Editor:	Michelle Moore
Book Designer/ Desktop Publisher:	Emil Yanos
Production Assistant:	Nathan Johanson
Indexer:	Ted Laux
Cover Designer:	Joanna Kim Gladden/Design Site
Cover Illustrator:	Mike Miller

SYBEX is a registered trademark of SYBEX Inc.

TRADEMARKS: SYBEX has attempted throughout this book to distinguish proprietary trademarks from descriptive terms by following the capitalization style used by the manufacturer.

Every effort has been made to supply complete and accurate information. However, SYBEX assumes no responsibility for its use, nor for any infringement of the intellectual property rights of third parties which would result from such use.

Photographs and illustrations used in this book have been downloaded from publicly accessible file archives and are used in this book for news reportage purposes only to demonstrate the variety of graphics resources available via electronic access. The source of each photograph or illustration is identified. Text and images available over the Internet may be subject to copyright and other rights owned by third parties. Online availability of text and images does not imply that they may be reused without the permission of rights holders, although the Copyright Act does permit certain unauthorized reuse as fair use under 17 U.S.C. Section 107. Care should be taken to ensure that all necessary rights are cleared prior to reusing material distributed over the Internet. Information about reuse rights is available from the institutions who make their materials available over the Internet.

Library of Congress Card Number: 95-71025

ISBN: 0-7821-1803-8

Manufactured in the United States of America

10 9 8 7 6 5 4 3 2 1

To all the young navigators (of all ages) who use the Internet for promoting peace in our global community

Acknowledgments

A book is a collaborative effort even if the author locks herself in a room to write it. A book about the Internet probably contains more contributions from more people than any other kind of book. Thank you to all the people I've never even met who shared URLs online, to the folks who have built fascinating sites in this new medium, and to all who work to keep the Internet open and free. At Sybex, many thanks to Brenda Kienan, who gave me the opportunity to explore the Internet and bring together interesting places in this book; to Malcolm Faulds for shepherding the project, and especially to Pat Coleman, whose careful and helpful editing prodded me to convey what I really wanted to say. Thanks to many colleagues for sharing sites, especially Deneen Frazier, Steve Klein, Bob Shayler, Rick Phelan, Rob King, and Ian Jukes. Huge piles of thanks to Joni Podolsky for her organizational work and to Peter Hutcher for lots and lots of time and space. Thanks to Bonnie Marks, David Thornburg, and especially Robert Burger for support and encouragement. A special thank-you to John Lytler, creator of Leeder O. Men, who gave permission for his original artwork to be included in this book. And to all those folks whose names I don't even know, thanks again for making the Internet such an intriguing place to visit.

Table of Contents

Introduction

Did you know that you can participate in a drumming concert, get information about the hiking trails at the Grand Canyon, see great works of art, or learn Italian right now at your computer? Through an Internet connection, you can do all these things and a whole lot more.

WHAT'S INSIDE?

The book is divided into two parts. Part One gives you information about what you'll need and how to become part of the online world. It describes Internet tools and discusses online rules and conventions. A glossary of the terms used in this book is at the end of Part One.

Part Two gets to the fun stuff. You'll find addresses and descriptions of more than 200 online sites. When you travel on vacation, you're probably interested in what you can see and do in new places and the people you'll meet. The Internet opens the whole world to online explorers, and I guarantee you'll find intriguing people and places there. You'll probably never visit another place that changes so fast. Before this book went to press, all the sites listed in the book were visited by at least two people. I can just about guarantee that by the time you take a look, a few sites will have disappeared, some will have new addresses, and others will have changed completely. You'll also find sites that weren't around when I was collecting the ones in this book. That's one thing that's so exciting about the Internet. It's always changing, and there's always a new, interesting place to discover. Perhaps you'll even add your own work to the online collection.

WHAT DOES THAT MEAN?

You'll find some icons that point to different kinds of information as you look through this book.

Notes tell you a little bit more about what you've just read or point out something of interest.

Tips offer some advice or suggest something you might do.

Warnings caution you about something, such as not to give out your phone number or home address online.

These next icons relate to the sites in Part Two. Each icon indicates a particular kind of site, that is, it tells you which online tool you'll need to get to the site. (You'll find information about what the tools do in Part One.)

The Web icon indicates that this site can be found on the World Wide Web using a Web browser such as Netscape or Mosaic. These days, you'll probably spend more time on the Web than on any other part of the Internet.

The Slow Link icon indicates that it may take a long time for the site to load onto your screen, but it's worth the wait!

The Gopher icon tells you that you'll be connecting to a site using a special tool developed at the University of Minnesota.

The Telnet icon lets you know you'll be getting to a different computer than the one you're using.

The FTP icon indicates you'll be getting to a site that lets you download files or pictures to your computer.

The Author's Pick icon says you've come to one of my favorite Internet sites. I've chosen it because it's beautiful to look at, well designed, contains a lot of useful information, or offers an opportunity to do something special.

NEXT STEPS

In this book, I've tried to present a variety of sources to get you started on what's out there. It's a small sampling of possibilities. Your explorations of the Internet will take you around the world and beyond. You'll meet kids from other countries, see what the astronauts see, and have a chance to share your writing or drawings with the world. You'll soon get to places you won't find in this (or any other) book, because they'll be so new that no one has had time to write about them. You can build collections of addresses and share them with friends. You'll soon be a seasoned Internet traveler, ready to tell friends about your discoveries. So let's begin.

Part One:
The Basics

1

About the Internet

The big news these days is about the Internet. In newspapers, magazines, television shows, and books, you see all kinds of discussion about the Information Superhighway (the Internet) and what it means to you.

The following list describes a few of the things you can do on the Internet:

◆ Look at NASA pictures directly from space

◆ Share your writing with others around the world

◆ Visit a museum thousands of miles from where you live while sitting at your computer

Until recently, getting to the Internet was often difficult, and once you were there, finding what you were looking for was tough too. Since the advent of the *World Wide Web* and software called *Web browsers* (see Figure 1.1), both things have become much easier.

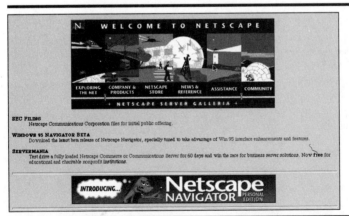

Figure 1.1:
This is the first screen you'll see when you open the Web browser called Netscape, version 1.1N.

But you need more than a browser. You need a connection that allows you access to the World Wide Web, and you'll find many *service providers* (the companies or organizations that provide you with an online account) willing to make you good deals if you'll use them as your Internet access point. How you can get connected, which kinds of connections to consider, and what you want to do when you get there are all topics we explore in this section. If you haven't already, you're about to join millions of travelers on the vast network of networks called the Internet.

No one knows exactly how many people are online. Some say more than 20 million, with 100,000 joining every month. Whatever the number, the Internet and its resources are a main topic of conversation almost everywhere you go.

WHAT'S IT LIKE OUT THERE?

The Internet provides lots of possibilities for exploration and interaction. Most people talk about three features:

- e-mail

- resources

- conferences

Let's look at each of them.

E-Mail Similar to writing a letter and sending it through the postal service (now called *snail mail,* or messages that you need a stamp to send), *e-mail* (messages that are sent electronically) is usually a one-to-one activity. Even when a whole class of students is writing to another class, each person is probably writing to one other person. One thing that's special about e-mail is that it doesn't matter when you write your letter and send it. It will be waiting for your friend on his or her system whenever your friend decides to get it. Your friend can write you right back or do so at another time. E-mail travels quickly through the system of connected computers that make up the Internet. Depending on the route it takes, e-mail generally gets from the sender's machine to where it's going within a few minutes or a few hours.

A Little Internet History

In the 1960s, the United States Department of Defense started exploring possibilities for a national communications system that could withstand nuclear attack. The scientists and engineers involved reasoned that the system should be *distributed*, or connected by computers that were not physically near one another, rather than *centralized*, or all in one place, so that if one part of the communications system were destroyed, other parts would survive, and communication could continue. No one controlled the system; it was open to those who could get access (a very small group of government people at the beginning). Out of this process, the Advanced Research Projects Agency (ARPA) developed a decentralized network of computers, which became known as ARPAnet. I'm happy to report that the network was never used for the purpose for which it was designed, and other people soon became interested in the possibilities it offered. Researchers at colleges and universities saw the value of being able to keep in close touch with colleagues working far away, and they began to join the network. Funded primarily through federal monies, what we know today as the Internet evolved. Soon other people and organizations set up their own networks and connected them to the existing global one. The number of Internet connections began to expand tremendously. Commercial services such as CompuServe, America Online, and Prodigy set up their own networks, and for a fee, subscribers could enjoy what each service offered, but couldn't communicate between services or with other Internet users. Eventually these services added Internet electronic mail, and now all have full Internet access. During the last few years, interest in the Internet has grown tremendously. More services and access are available from a variety of providers, and more and more people are joining the online world and sharing resources, ideas, and information (see Figure 1.2).

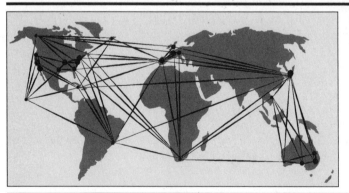

Figure 1.2:
People all over the world are connected through the Internet.

Resources Access to information *resources* such as graphics, sounds, or video is another exciting reason to use the Internet. You can find and gather these resources through Internet connections. When you visit the Louvre Museum in Paris, France, or the Library of Congress in Washington, DC, via telecommunications, you aren't in touch with a specific person as you are when you use e-mail, but rather with the wonderful artwork and print resources these institutions provide. Through your computer, you can look at pictures, read books, view short movies, or bring any or all of these back to your own computer to use after you've closed your telecommunications connection, or gone *offline.*

> *With your Web browser, you'll find that the possibilities of places to visit online are nearly endless.*

With your Web browser, you'll find that the possibilities of places to visit online are nearly endless. Whether you're interested in the latest sports stats, how to make a particular quilting pattern, or what kids at other schools are doing, you'll be able to find Internet sites that can satisfy your curiosity. The sites you'll find in Part Two of this book will connect you with resources all over the world on a number of topics.

Conferences The third kind of popular Internet activity has various names: conferences, forums, newsgroups, and discussion centers, for example. Let's stick with *conferences* for now. During an online conference, you can hear from others about a topic and let them know what you think as well.

In a face-to-face discussion, a number of people get together to talk about a particular topic, for example, which team will win the Super Bowl or who might be elected the next president of the United States. Everyone's opinion is important, and people take turns sharing. The same is true in an online conference. Anyone can start a discussion by *posting,* or typing, a question, a comment, an idea, or a challenge. Anyone else who comes across the posting can respond, and the original posting, along with all the responses, are there for whomever is interested in following the discussion. Some conferences are moderated, and some are not. A *moderated* conference is one in which someone takes responsibility for posting the original message, monitoring the responses, and making sure the participants follow reasonable guidelines in their discussion. *Unmoderated* conferences are those in which anyone can post a message and in which just about anything goes. Of course, if participants complain to the *system administrator* (the person who runs or oversees the operation of an online service), he or she may ask the people who have posted offensive messages to stop and may even kick them off the system. Although the system administrator may or may not live in the same city where the telecommunication system's *server* (the powerful computer that holds all the information that is part of an online service) is placed, he or she has special privileges that allow such activities as monitoring discussions and denying access to the system.

Just as there are rules for driving cars safely or behaving appropriately in school, there are expectations about how people act when they're online. We'll talk more about online manners, or netiquette, *a bit later.*

The Internet is an amazing place. Because it grew from a system with no one in charge, it has grown with little or no order to it. Most people who sign up for an online account and *log on*, or check in, to their system are as interested in sharing resources, ideas, and information as they are in getting such material from others. There is a lot to look at, sift through, and explore, with more appearing every day. A little later in this section (see *Tools for the Trip*), we'll talk about some tools that make it possible to locate what you're looking for more easily. For now, just realize that you'll spend some time now and again exploring. And isn't that what travel is all about? You never know what might turn up around the next bend in a road or at the next Internet site.

How Do You Join?

You have some options to consider when you decide that you want to get online and explore the Internet.

SERVICE PROVIDERS

First, you'll think about what you want to do online. A variety of Internet service providers offer different kinds of access. One way to think about providers is to look at whether they provide some things for you to do or explore or simply give you access to the Internet. For example, some commercial online service providers, such as America Online, CompuServe, and Prodigy, provide a multitude of activities, from letting you play games, to reading online magazines, to providing places where you can write to other users who happen to be online at the same time. When you sign up, that is, when you agree to subscribe to a service for a fee, these companies provide you with software that will only work on their system. For example, you may have found advertisements including diskettes in Internet magazines at the newsstand that invite you to sign up for America Online. When you install that software on your computer, it connects you only to America Online. CompuServe, Prodigy, e-World, and others provide software for their systems when you join them.

One way to think about providers is to look at whether they provide some things for you to do or explore or simply give you access to the Internet.

The systems of some service providers are designed to meet the needs of a specific group. For example, the information on the DCCG (Disabled Children's Computer Group) Bulletin Board in Berkeley, California, will primarily be of interest to people with disabilities and their care providers. To get to an online site such as DCCG, you'll need to know its phone number and have telecommunications software and your modem already set up. (We'll be talking about all the things you need to go online in a later section.) Bulletin boards are services that often provide information of interest to a specific group of people, and electronic mail within the system may or may not be available. Electronic bulletin boards are similar to the kind you find on the walls at school or in libraries. You can go there to read notices, but you can't respond immediately to what you see, as you can with an e-mail message.

Yet others, designed by and for a particular audience, such as a community or an educational group, might offer Internet access as well as links to resources on other systems the audience finds valuable. These service providers are generally small or local groups, sometimes funded by their parent organizations. You won't have to pay to join them, but your access may be limited to that particular service.

Another kind of Internet service provider offers access to the Internet but no direct services. You won't see a menu of options to choose from when you connect; you'll go directly to the Internet site you want. Examples of such service providers are BBN Planet and Netcom. When you have an account with them, you connect by means of telecommunications software that you purchase or already own, such as Microsoft Works, Eudora (a popular e-mail program), or Netscape (a well-known Web browser). If for some reason you decide to change from one of these service providers to another, you can still use the same software: Microsoft Works, Eudora, and Netscape work with all these kinds of systems, depending on the kind of connection you have (see the *VT-100 Connection* and *SLIP or PPP Connection* sections).

> *Perhaps the main difference among these has to do with how much you want to do on your own and what you can afford.*

We've talked a bit about three types of services: commercial, bulletin board, and Internet access-only. Perhaps the main difference among these has to do with how much you want to do on your own and what you can afford. It's fun to be on a popular system where lots of places to go are already set up. On the other hand, if you know how to navigate around the Internet and don't want some of the extra services you'll never use, you'll do fine with a provider that simply gets you onto the Internet. You might begin by taking a look at Appendix B, where you'll find a current listing of Internet service providers.

COSTS

Table 1.1 will give you an idea of how much it costs to connect with some of the larger, more well-known Internet service providers. You might also check the newsstands. Often, you'll find a publication that lists service providers for your area. Again, talk with friends, experiment with some free-trial offers, and then make your decision.

As you can see, along with their monthly rates, some companies charge an hourly fee to use or start service. Depending on what you want to do and how much time you think you'll need, you'll decide what works best.

Table 1.1 Here are some examples of typical Internet service costs.			
Service Provider	**Monthly Rate**	**Hourly Rate**	**Startup Fee**
America Online	$9.95 (includes 5 hrs)	$2.95/hour	None
CompuServe	$9.95 (includes 5 hrs)	$2.95/hour	None
Delphi	$10/month (4 hours), $20/month (20 hours), $3.00/month for Internet	None	$19.00
GEnie	$4.95	$6/hour evenings and weekends; $12.50/hour during business hours	None
Netcom	$19.50	None	$25.00
Prodigy	$9.95 (includes 5 hrs)	25 cents/minute	$25.00
The Well	$15.00	$2.00	None
Microsoft Network	$4.95 (includes 3 hrs)	$2.50/hour	None

PHONE-LINE CONNECTION

Internet connections fall into two main categories—*direct* and *dial-up*. In a *direct connection*, your computer is part of a network that includes expensive and specialized hardware and software that links directly to its service provider. Your school might have such a system, or your parents might have access to such a system at work.

In a *dial-up connection,* you use your regular telephone line to connect with a service provider. Anyone can get a dial-up connection. For the purposes of this book, we're talking about a dial-up connection in which the set-up includes:

◆   a computer (any computer)

◆   communications software

◆   a modem

◆   an online connection

◆   access to a phone line

◆   a reason for going to all this trouble

Let's take a look at each of these items.

YOUR COMPUTER

Whether you have a Macintosh, an IBM, a Compaq, an Apple IIgs, or just about any other computer, you can telecommunicate. You can connect through your modem and the phone lines with everyone else who has Internet access, no matter what sort of machine they have. Because messages you send and information you get online goes through your Internet service provider's computer, you don't have to worry about what anyone else is using. Over the years, consistent ways of doing things, or *protocols*, have been developed.

What Are Internet Protocols?

Protocols are the rules that online systems have agreed to follow so that information can be exchanged between them. It's as if your computer knows what it's supposed to do because it follows a script or a set of instructions. For example, you know what to do when you visit a library because you've learned the procedure. If you want to borrow a book, you know you need a library card to check it out. You take the book to the desk for check-out, you find out when it's due, and you return it on time or pay a fine. In the same way, a standard procedure, called *TCP/IP* (Transmission Control Protocol/Internet Protocol) is used on the Internet.

Thus, my Macintosh can understand messages sent from your DOS machine, and vice versa.

 Although it isn't necessary to use Microsoft Windows on your DOS machine, you'll have an easier and more enjoyable time exploring the Internet if you do. Rather than typing in text, you'll be able to move around by pointing and clicking. If you have a color monitor, you'll be able to enjoy the great graphics even more.

YOUR COMMUNICATIONS SOFTWARE

If you use a program such as Microsoft Works or ClarisWorks, you've already got communications software; it's part of the program. When you buy a modem, software is often included in the box. And many *shareware* and commercial packages are available as well.

What Is Shareware?

Shareware is a program that is made available by its developer on a trial basis at no cost to you. If you like the product and will continue to use it, you are requested to send money to the developer. In that way, you register with the person who wrote the program and will often get news of updates and further developments

You may want to start with the software that you already have on your computer or with the software that came with your modem. See how what you've already got works before you go looking for something else. If you need other features or hear about other interesting software from friends on- or offline, you'll have some basis for comparison if you decide to switch. Of course, if you select a commercial Internet service provider such as America Online, CompuServe, or Prodigy, you'll use the software they provide.

YOUR MODEM

A modem is the device that takes the type of information the computer uses and changes it into the type of information that a phone line can handle and vice versa. The word *modem* is a contraction of *mo*dulator/*dem*odulator, which refers to the job a modem performs. Modems come in two forms— *internal* and *external*. An internal modem fits inside your computer;

an external modem attaches to your computer through a cable. Take a look at Figure 1.3 to see some examples of modems.

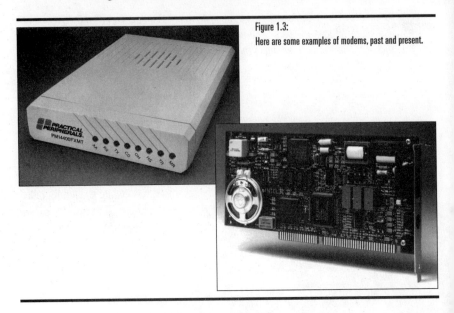

Figure 1.3:
Here are some examples of modems, past and present.

YOUR ONLINE CONNECTIONS

With all this hardware and software, you're ready to connect to the online world with an account through a service provider. The two common kinds of connections are:

◆ VT-100 (also called *text-based* or *line mode*)

◆ SLIP or PPP

VT-100 CONNECTION

When you log on to a system with a VT-100 connection, you'll see menus. You move around through a series of menus by typing in numbers or letters until you get to where you want to be. For example, Figure 1.4 shows the main menu of the Telis system.

```
        Telis Main Menu              Tue Jul 11 11:33:28 PDT 1995
    [a] Access UNIX command line (restricted)
    [b] Bulletins and News from Telis
    [c] Chat (with Telis folk and IRC)
    [d] Databases (CalTIP, ERIC, Telis, etc.)
    [e] EMail (Electronic Mail) - PINE full screen
    [f] FTP Services (files & information from everywhere)
    [g] Gopherspace (find files & information from everywhere)
    [h] Help (help using Telis and the Internet)
    [l] Lynx (text-based World Wide Web browser)
    [n] Newsgroups (conferences and discussions)
    [r] Resources from Organizations
    [s] Search the Internet (keywords)
    [t] Telnet outside Telis (go to other systems)
    [u] User Information (names and resumes) and Password Change
    [w] Finger (who/what/where)
    [z] User File Operations (zmodem upload and download)
    [p] Telis Logon Menu

    [q] Quit this Telis Session and Log-Out

Your choice: █
```

Figure 1.4:
Telis is an example of a VT-100, or text-based connection.

If you select option E, you can look at your e-mail. The other options will take you to services that the Telis system offers. At any rate, the way you move around in a VT-100 or text-based connection is by reading words and indicating your choices by typing a letter or a number or using the arrow keys ($\uparrow$, $\downarrow$, $\leftarrow$, and $\rightarrow$) and the ↵ key.

Buying a Modem

When you buy a modem, you want to pay attention to the *baud* or *bps rate*—the speed at which information travels through it. (The letters *bps* stand for *bits per second*.) The higher the baud rate, the faster information travels. When you're online, you can be accumulating phone charges, which you (or perhaps your parents) have to pay when the phone bill arrives. In some areas, even local calls can cost money, so you'll want to be online for as short a time as possible. My old 300-baud modem doesn't work on most systems any more, and even if it did, it would be very slow. A 1200- or 2400-baud modem will work with some services, but if you're buying a modem, you'll want a faster one, with a baud rate of at least 14,400 bps; 28,800 bps is even better. Modems vary in price, but you should be able to find a 14,400-baud modem for less than $100.00. You'll need a 14,400-baud modem if you're going to get a SLIP or PPP connection (see the next section for an explanation) and want to see or download the wonderful videos and graphics available on the Internet.

SLIP OR PPP CONNECTION

The other type of connection is called a *SLIP* (Serial Line Internet Protocol) or *PPP* (Point-to-Point Protocol) connection. SLIP and PPP connections are faster and more powerful than a VT-100 connection. When you are connected via SLIP or PPP, you'll see screens that include *icons* (small pictures). You select these icons to get to where you want to be and do what you want to do. These screens are the *interface* between you at your computer and the computers on the Internet to which you're connecting. With a SLIP or PPP connection, you can use *graphical interface* software (see Figure 1.5) and a mouse to point and click on selections. With a graphical interface, instead of reading words and pressing letters or numbers to get to where you want to go, for the most part you click on pictures, text, or icons.

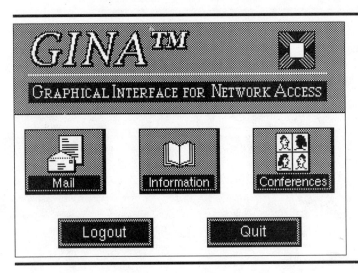

Figure 1.5: GINA software illustrates a point-and-click graphical interface, which requires a SLIP connection.

With a SLIP or PPP connection, you can see, play, and download graphics, video, and sounds. Your access to the information is generally easier and faster than in a text-based connection.

You will need at least a 9600-baud modem to use a graphical interface well, and 14,400- or 28,800-baud modems are even better.

Some services, such as California's CORE+, offer both VT-100 and SLIP or PPP access, at least for now. It's usually cheaper to go with the VT-100 connection, but I think you're going to want the power behind a SLIP or PPP connection if you want to explore the Internet's riches quickly and easily.

After you've talked with friends, maybe tried out a few services (perhaps from the list in Appendix B), and decided on the one that's appropriate for you, you'll sign up, pay the fees, and get your *login*, or online address, and password.

It might be possible to get a connection through your school, depending on the terms of the use agreement between your school and the system it has an account with, as well as the acceptable use policy your school has developed. Acceptable use documents spell out how the system is to be used by teachers and students and what constitutes acceptable online behavior.

ACCESS TO A PHONE LINE

Although nice, it's not necessary to have a special phone line just for telecommunications. You can use a single phone line both for talking and for your online sessions. If you share a phone line with your family, you'll want to work out with them when and for how long you can use the phone for your online sessions. Just as if you were calling a friend who lives nearby, when you're online, those trying to reach you or other family members will get a busy signal.

*If you have Call Waiting on your phone, you'll want to disable it before you connect to your online service. If you don't, you'll lose your modem connection when a call comes in. Often you can simply dial *70 to do this before you set your modem to make its call. Check with your phone company to be sure. And some online services show you a little box that you can check to disable Call Waiting automatically every time you sign on. After you've disconnected from your online service, Call Waiting will automatically reset.*

A REASON FOR GOING TO ALL THIS TROUBLE

If you've never had an online conversation with someone you don't know who lives half a world away, or looked at NASA satellite pictures on your own computer at the same time the Goddard Space Center sees them, or gotten comments from people who saw your artwork at an online gallery, you may not understand what all the excitement is about. I'll bet there's something on the Internet you'll be delighted to find. At least give it a chance. Ask a friend to take you on a tour or see if your local library offers free online exploration. When you're convinced and have an account, I think you'll be interested in some software applications in the next section that make online life easier.

A Question of Internet Access

Most service providers offer their subscribers some variation of access to the three Internet activities we talked about—e-mail, resources, and conferences. Virtually all include Internet e-mail. So for the cost of a local phone call, you can exchange messages with anyone literally anywhere in the world who also has an Internet e-mail account.

Regarding resources and conferences, however, there's a different story. Commercial providers select a number of features to offer. These features are available only to their subscribers. For example, if you have an account on CompuServe, you can access a feature called Fun & Games, but you cannot access this CompuServe feature through America Online. At this time, Prodigy, America Online, and CompuServe have Web browsers that *do* allow their subscribers to explore the Internet fully. Other providers offer e-mail and may or may not allow full Internet access. When you have full internet access, you can use the tools we'll talk about a little later to enter other systems, download files, and so on. It all depends on what you're looking for. Explore a few of the systems that offer free trials. Talk with friends. Decide what you want to do online. Then make your decision to subscribe.

Tools for the Trip

You may have heard about tools for finding and getting information on the Internet. We're going to look at a few of them now:

- Gopher

- Telnet

- FTP

- World Wide Web

Unix is the basic software that used to run all Internet machines, and many people found it difficult to learn and use. However, technology has progressed so far these days that even if the online service you're linked into uses Unix, you don't have to know Unix commands. The service provider's interface takes care of all that for you.

Just as real gophers may dig tunnels in your lawn, the Gopher software program creates paths between servers so that you can get to files, documents, or even other computers easily, without having to know the address.

THE GOPHER TOOL

Gopher is a software tool that was developed at the University of Minnesota, home of the Golden Gophers. Just as real gophers may dig tunnels in your lawn, the Gopher software program creates paths between servers so that you can get to files, documents, or even other computers easily, without having to know the address. For example, as you can see in Figure 1.6, the KQED Learning Link system lists nine Gopher connections (letters A-K). If you want to connect to the NASA Goddard Space Flight Center, all you have to do is press the letter **A**, and you'll be immediately connected, thanks to the Gopher tool. From there, you can select from among the files and documents available at that site in the same way—by choosing a letter. You can just as easily connect to C-SPAN, KIDLINK, or The Hub at TERC. Each of these sites has a specific Internet address, but you don't have to find it or type it. The KQED Learning Link system administrator has decided on the Gopher sites he thinks his subscribers will find valuable, and those are the ones listed.

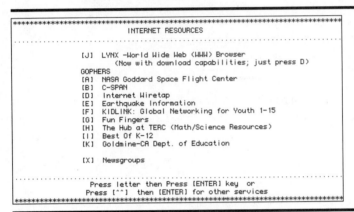

```
****************************************************************
                    INTERNET RESOURCES
...............................................................

    [J]  LYNX -World Wide Web (WWW) Browser
            (Now with download capabilities; just press D)
    GOPHERS
    [A]  NASA Goddard Space Flight Center
    [B]  C-SPAN
    [D]  Internet Wiretap
    [E]  Earthquake Information
    [F]  KIDLINK: Global Networking for Youth 1-15
    [G]  Fun Fingers
    [H]  The Hub at TERC (Math/Science Resources)
    [I]  Best Of K-12
    [K]  Goldmine-CA Dept. of Education

    [X]  Newsgroups

...............................................................
        Press letter then Press [ENTER] key  or
        Press [^^] then [ENTER] for other services
****************************************************************
```

Figure 1.6:
KQED's Learning Link provides Gopher access to a variety of resources.

The Gopher tool can only take paths to servers or sections of servers that are open to the public. That means you never have to know a password to get access. Wherever those paths have been built, you can travel them.

You can use the Gopher tool in several ways to get to where you want to go. If you have a VT-100 connection, you'll see a screen something like Figure 1.6. You'll know you're in *Gopherspace* (those sites on the Internet where the Gopher software tool is being used) because you'll be able to select from a list of Gophers, or see a heading such as the one in Figure 1.7: Internet Gopher Information Client 2.0. Then all you need to do is type the letter **o** and the address of where you want to go and you'll be there, because your system has made the Gopher tool available. For example, if I decide I want to get to Harlem, New York's Ralph Bunche School Gopher—a site that isn't listed in the CORE Gopher—I type **o** and then fill in the Gopher address (ralphbunche.rbs.edu) across from Hostname (see Figure 1.7). When I press ↵, I'll be connected directly to the Ralph Bunche School Gopher and can make further selections.

If you have a SLIP or PPP connection, you can use another tool called TurboGopher (for the Macintosh) or PC Graphics III (for DOS computers),

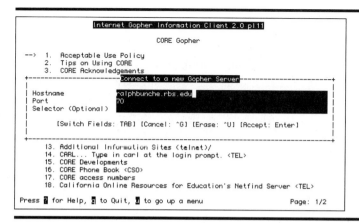

Figure 1.7:
When you type the
o command, you can
open a path to any
Gopher site if you
know the address.

which lets you get to any interesting Gopher address you've found. In this case, you don't have to worry about whether your service provider has set up paths to the Gophers you want to reach. You can install the software on your computer and use it when you need it. Figure 1.8 shows a typical TurboGopher screen.

If you're using the World Wide Web, you can also type a Gopher address and get to the site quickly (see the *World Wide Web* section for more details).

The Gopher tool makes traveling in Gopherspace a breeze. Universities, libraries, and other organizations with a lot of information to share add themselves to Gopherspace all the time. Using Gopher, you can get to files that answer questions you're curious about. You can take a look at them, and if you want, you can save them to your computer. Now if you come across a Gopher address you'd like to check out, you'll have an idea about how to get to it.

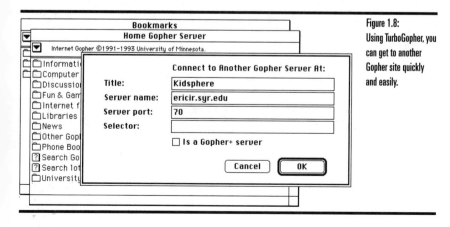

Figure 1.8:
Using TurboGopher, you
can get to another
Gopher site quickly
and easily.

THE TELNET TOOL

Telnet is a tool that lets you operate another computer remotely from your computer. Your service provider may offer Telnet access. For example, Telnet is one of the features that I can use on the Telis system. I can log on to my account on the Telis system in California (where I live) by making a local phone call. Then I can telnet to a computer in Alaska (where I also have an account) and access all the features of *that* system as if I were calling locally. The phone charges will be local, even though I've made quite a long distance connection.

Recently I attended a conference in Baltimore, Maryland. Computers were set up so that attendees could get their e-mail. First I opened a Telnet session by clicking on the button on the screen that said "Telnet." Next I typed **telis.org**, which is the Internet address of the server where my Telis account resides. Then I saw the same screen I would have seen if I had been at home and had my modem dial the Telis system. I entered my login and password and soon started reading and answering my e-mail.

Some systems allow you to telnet to them only if you have an account. When you use those systems, you'll give your account name, number, and password. Other systems are open and let you log in calling yourself "guest" or "anonymous." Then you can make selections as if you started your online session by calling directly; you have full access.

As with Gopher sessions, you can go where you want in a few ways. If you've got a VT-100 connection (as I do on Telis and KQED Learning Link), you'll be able to Telnet in from another system in the way I've described above. If you have a SLIP or PPP account, you can use a software program called NCSA Telnet, which is available for both Macintosh and DOS machines. Figure 1.9 shows what happens when you activate NCSA Telnet. After you type an address (ousd.k12.ca.us in this case), you'll be asked for your login. Either type your login for that system or log on as guest or anonymous.

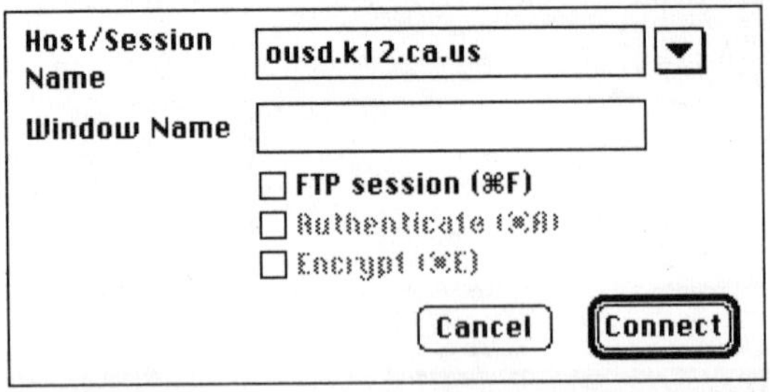

| Host/Session Name | ousd.k12.ca.us ▼ |
| Window Name | |

☐ **FTP session (⌘F)**
☐ Authenticate (⌘A)
☐ Encrypt (⌘E)

[Cancel] [**Connect**]

Figure 1.9:
NCSA Telnet lets you connect to other systems quickly and easily.

NCSA Telnet is a public domain *program (that is, it is free, and anyone who wants to can copy it) you can use if you have a SLIP or PPP connection to get to other computers fast and easily. You can download it for your Macintosh or DOS machine from the World Wide Web at* http:// www.ncsa.uiuc.edu *or via FTP at* ftp.ncsa.uiuc.edu. *(Go either to the Mac or the PC directory, depending on the type of computer you have.) World Wide Web and FTP are explained below.*

THE FTP TOOL

FTP stands for *File Transfer Protocol* and is a tool you can use to transfer a file from your computer to another or from another computer to your own. Transferring files has not always been easy for several reasons. Your computer and the one you want to transfer files between may not be compatible. Also, you have to know the exact address of where you're going and pretty much what you want, because you won't be able to open the files and take a look at them before you download them. But if you do determine what you want and where you need to go, you can use FTP to get that file, graphic, or document to your computer quickly.

As with Telnet and Gopher, software has been developed that makes the transfer process run more smoothly. If you have a SLIP or PPP connection, you can use software called Fetch for the Macintosh or WS FTP for Windows. Figure 1.10 shows an example of Fetch at work. First you activate Fetch, and when you enter the name of the FTP site you want to reach, Fetch takes you there. Now you download the files you want.

You can FTP Fetch from gated.cornell.edu. *Go to the directory PUB/VIDEO/ FETCH and to the file named FETCH_2.1.HQX. You can download WS FTP for Windows via Gopher at* gopher.forestry.umn.edu:1001/11/pub/dos/Windows/winsock.

Gopher, Telnet, and FTP are valuable tools that have made exploring and using the Internet easier over the years. However, with the advent of the World Wide Web and Web browsers, life on the Internet is easier still and much more interesting.

THE WORLD WIDE WEB

Recently, the most exciting development on the Internet has been the growth of the World Wide Web and the development of Web browsers. You may have heard of software programs such as Mosaic, Netscape, or MacWeb. These are

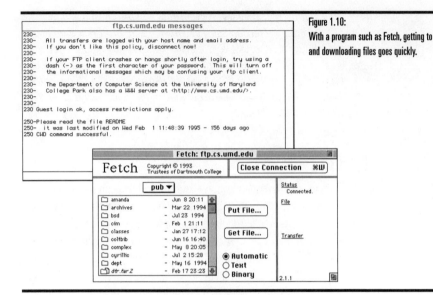

Figure 1.10:
With a program such as Fetch, getting to and downloading files goes quickly.

all Web browsers. They're graphical interface programs that make exploring the Internet fun and easy. They take the plain text that used to be all you saw on the Internet and show it to you in the form of attractive fonts and images on pages. Some text and some images are highlighted. By pointing and clicking on the highlights, you can follow an amazing trail through an array of resources. Figure 1.11 shows you an example of a home page I got to by using Netscape. A home page is the first screen you'll see when you get to an Internet site through the World Wide Web. It's sort of like the first page in a book. Any highlighted words, lines, or images you see on the home page will take you to another page when you click on them. The home page usually offers a sort of "table of contents" for what you'll find at that site.

> *By pointing and clicking on the highlights, you can follow an amazing trail through an array of resources.*

More and more Web browsers are being developed even as you are reading this. Some work faster than others, and some might even have trouble getting to a particular site.

Figure 1.11:
The home page for the Oakland Unified School District in Oakland, California

HYPERTEXT LINKS

Text and images that are highlighted or underlined or sometimes highlighted and underlined are called *hypertext links*. Clicking on them takes you to another place on the Web. (Sometimes clicking on a link takes you to a bigger image of what you're already looking at or plays a sound or video.)

Hypertext links are created through a language called HTML, *hypertext markup language*. To produce all the beautiful pages you'll see on the World Wide Web, publishers use HTML coding to indicate where and what size the text should be, where pictures should go, and which hypertext links to add. You can find books that teach you the codes and how to use them.

> *To produce all the beautiful pages you'll see on the World Wide Web, publishers use HTML coding.*

Some classes are being offered that let you practice making your own pages. You may even find some of these classes online. Take a look at the *Tools* section of this book for some places on the Internet to get all kinds of help in writing your own HTML documents.

Figure 1.12 shows the same page in two ways: with the actual HTML coding, and the document it produces that you see on the World Wide Web through a Web browser.

```
<HEAD>
<TITLE> Oakland Unified School District Home Page </TITLE>
<BODY>

<table border=5 cellpadding=2><LEFT><tr><td> <IMG SRC="ousd2.gif"
HEIGHT=115 WIDTH=250 BORDER=2> <IMG SRC="oak.gif"
HEIGHT=115 WIDTH=140 BORDER=2><RIGHT></TD></TR></RIGHT></TABLE>
<p><b>Oakland Unified School District * 1025 2nd Ave, Oakland, CA, USA 94606</b>
<P>
The Mission of the OUSD network is to enable the OUSD community to use
telecomputing facilities to enhance and support teach
the exchange of creative ideas, resources, research an
cooperate and collaborate in a socially responsible m
learners in a global society.
<P>
This info-highway onramp is permanently "under cons
welcomed.
<hr size=4 align=left width=75%>
This weeks' highlight <blink> <A
HREF="http://ousd.k12.ca.us/summer.classes.html">Su
Courses</a></blink></B> with online registration for
<hr size=4 align=left width=75%>
<L1><A HREF="ousd.info.html">Check <b>Here</b> For U
Info</A><BR>
<L1><A HREF="ousd.schls.html">What's happening at ou
<L1><A HREF="curric.res.html">Curriculum Resources<
<L1><A HREF="info.res.html">Information Resources</
<L1><A HREF="com.res.html">Oakland Area Community
<L1><A HREF="way.cool.html">Way Cool Stuff</A><BR>
<hr size=4 align=left width=75%>
<i>Last updated 6/11/95</i><BR>
For more information contact <A HREF="PeterH/ph.pag
```

Figure 1.12:

The home page of the Oakland Unified School District seen in two ways: how it looks written in HTML coding (left), and how you and others see it on the World Wide Web (below)

Oakland Unified School District * 1025 2nd Ave, Oakland, CA, USA 94606

The Mission of the OUSD network is to enable the OUSD community to use telecomputing facilities to enhance and support teaching and learning; to promote the exchange of creative ideas, resources, research and general information; to cooperate and collaborate in a socially responsible manner; and to become active learners in a global society.

This info-highway onramp is permanently "under construction." Suggestions warmly welcomed.

This weeks' highlight Summer Macintosh Training Courses with online registration form.

Check **Here** For Useful Oakland USD Info
What's happening at our schools
Curriculum Resources
Information Resources
Oakland Area Community Resources
Way Cool Stuff

Last updated 6/11/95
For more information contact Peter Hutcher at 510.836.8253 or send e-mail to peter@ousd.k12.ca.us

This web server was installed by: Lloyd Internetworking

You can download Web browsers for Macintosh and Windows computers from the Internet.

To get Netscape, go to http://home.mcom.com/comprod/index.html or FTP to ftp.mcom.com, directory: NETSCAPE, file: either MAC or WINDOWS.

To get NCSA Mosaic for both Macintosh and Windows, go to http://www.ncsa.uiuc.edu. (You'll be able to download NCSA Mosaic for the proper platform depending on the type of computer you use to connect to the Web site.)

To get MacWeb for the Macintosh, go to http://galaxy.einet.net or FTP to ftp.einet.net, directory: /EINET/MAC/MACWEB, file: MACWEB.LATEST.SEA.HQX.

To get WinWeb for Windows, go to http://galaxy.einet.net or FTP to ftp.einet.net, directory: /EINET/PC/WINWEB, file: /EINET/PC/WINWEB/WINWEB.ZIP.

In a text-based system such as KQED's Learning Link, you know exactly where you're going. When you click on a Web link, you often don't know quite where you'll end up. For example, if I see a highlighted word such as NASA on a Web page that lists space science resources, I will probably find myself at the NASA home page, where I can click on other links that may keep me on their server or move me to another one.

You'll find lots of lists of places to go on the World Wide Web. To get where you want to go, find "open location" by clicking on the File menu. Then enter the address, or *URL*. (URL stands for uniform resource locator.) Just as your home address tells people where to find you, the URL for a site indicates where to find it on the Internet. In Part Two, you'll find URLs for all the sites in the book. For example, to get to the University of California's Museum of Paleontology on the Internet, you type its URL, which is http://ucmp1.berkeley.edu. You'll then see its home page, because you've arrived at the right address.

When you go to Web sites, you always start your address with http://. *When you go to a Gopher site, you start the address with* gopher://. *When you go to a Telnet site, you start the address with* telnet://. *When you go to an FTP site, you start the address with* ftp://. *This convention simplifies exploring the Internet.*

Incidentally, many text-based systems offer access to the World Wide Web through software such as the Lynx browser (see Figure 1.13). In this case, you'll see what looks like a text-based menu, but you're really getting the same hypertext links that you would get with the more powerful browsers. (In fact, if you compare Figure 1.11 with Figure 1.13, you notice that the pictures in Figure 1.11 each show up as [IMAGE] in Figure 1.13.)

You don't need a SLIP or PPP connection to use Lynx. However, you'll not be able to see the pictures, hear the sounds, or view the videos. You'll just get the written part. But if all that's available to you is a VT-100 connection that includes a Lynx browser, you can still find your way to a lot that's available on the World Wide Web.

```
                    Oakland Unified School District Home Page  (p1 of 2)

[IMAGE] [IMAGE]

Oakland Unified School District * 1025 2nd Ave, Oakland, CA, USA
94606
The Mission of the OUSD network is to enable the OUSD community to use
telecomputing facilities to enhance and support teaching and learning;
to promote the exchange of creative ideas, resources, research and
general information; to cooperate and collaborate in a socially
responsible manner; and to become active learners in a global society.


This info-highway onramp is permanently "under construction."
Suggestions warmly welcomed.


This weeks' highlight Summer Macintosh Training Courses with online
registration form.
-- press space for more, use arrow keys to move, '?' for help, 'q' to quit
 Arrow keys: Up and Down to move. Right to follow a link; Left to go back.
 H)elp O)ptions P)rint G)o M)ain screen Q)uit /=search [delete]=history list
```

Figure 1.13: Text-based Lynx browsers also offer World Wide Web access but without the pictures.

Local Customs

When you visit a foreign country, you'll get more out of your trip if you know something about the customs and the language. For example, you might find that nodding in response to a question doesn't always mean yes. Or you might find it important to bow instead of offering to shake hands. Or you might want to cover your head with a cap or scarf when you enter some holy places. Also, if you've ever tried to order food at a restaurant where the menu is written entirely in a language you don't read, you know how difficult that is. You might enjoy what you get, but you might also get a big surprise if you simply point to an unknown selection. Often guidebooks to foreign countries offer tips to travelers regarding their safety. Sometimes you even have to get vaccinations before you go.

The Internet has its own culture, and although the language of the Internet is mainly English, there are ways of saying and doing things that make the experience more comfortable for newbies.

The Internet has its own culture, and although the language of the Internet is mainly English, there are ways of saying and doing things that make the experience more comfortable for *newbies* (new users) and old timers alike. You won't have to get a shot from the doctor before you go online, and you don't need to worry about drinking the water or catching any local diseases, but you'll enjoy yourself more if you're clued in to the traditions.

As I've said before, sometimes when you're traveling on the Internet, you'll end up in completely unexpected places. You might stumble on exactly the resource you've been looking for or one that brings you exciting new ideas to think about. However, if you happen to come across material that upsets you, tell an adult about it. If you happen to get into a conversation with someone who is bothering you, leave that area of the Internet. Some systems have safeguards for their users. America Online, for example, tries to provide safe, interesting places for its users. If you are in a conference where someone is behaving inappropriately, for example, you can send mail to the system administrator, who will contact that person and ask him or her to stop. People who continue to bother people will no longer be allowed on the system. You're using a machine; it's under your control. You can always turn it off.

It's very important to keep your home phone number and address private— don't give them out online.

NETIQUETTE

Etiquette is a term that describes acceptable behavior in our society. Some rules seem old-fashioned and out of date, but some of them help us all get along better. For example, it's polite to say "Excuse me" if you bump into someone by accident. It's not absolutely necessary; the other person probably won't say or do anything if you don't, but saying the words makes a difference in the encounter between you and the other person. That Golden Rule

♦ Do unto others as you would have others do unto you

applies here. It's simply nice when people are pleasant to one another. The Internet is another place where people encounter people—strangers and friends—along with some interesting challenges. Over the years, online users have come up with some rules for online behavior, called *netiquette*. The main reason for abiding by these rules is so that you will be clear in your communication. When you communicate clearly, people will understand what you're asking and will want to help you, and they will want to share what they're doing with you.

Over the years, online users have come up with some rules for online behavior, called netiquette.

When you're writing e-mail messages, for example, you'll want to be clear about the questions you are answering. It can be very confusing if someone asks you a question and your response is something like "Yes." By the time the person who wrote you gets the reply, she may have forgotten the question, especially if she wrote to several people at the same time, asking a number of questions. With most e-mail systems, you can answer the message with a *reply* command, which lets you send a response directly back to the person who wrote you, as in Figure 1.14.

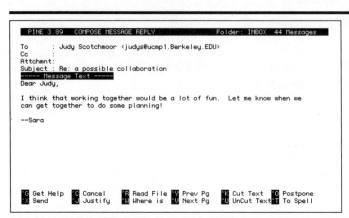

Figure 1.14:
When you use the
Reply command,
the mail system
automatically sets up
the To: and From: parts
of your message so
that all you have to do
is write.

You won't have to worry about addressing the message or entering a subject—those things will be done for you. You will also probably have the option of including your original message.

E-mail messages are most clear when they're written like a letter. It's good netiquette to start the message with "Dear" and to end it with some closing words and your name, as well as your e-mail address. Although your address shows up in the header of your message, it may get lost or become so embedded in other text that your friend may have a hard time figuring it out. Depending on your mail program, you may have the ability to add a *signature* to your messages. A signature usually includes the sender's name, e-mail address, and other information he or she wants everyone to see. It's good netiquette to keep signatures to three to five lines. Sometimes people include a quotation they like or a small picture composed of keyboard characters. Sometimes people surround the signature with asterisks (*) or other characters to set it off from the message. Figure 1.15 shows a few examples of signatures.

Because you never know what kind of computer other people online are using, you can't count on special characters showing up in your messages, even if you've put them in. Most computers on the Internet recognize what is called *ASCII*, which means American Standard Code for Information

```
Bob Shayler  -  bshayler@xxx.xxx  -or-  BobShayler@xxx.xxx
Teacher of Physics & Integrated Science - California State Telementor
"Schools exist for the benefit of Students, not the other way around"
///=========================================================\\\
    for a good time, connect with ftp://ftp.mcom.com/netscape/
\\\=========================================================///



                     @)--;--
           Judi Harris
  _  /|_^_      Department of Curriculum & Instruction
 \'o.o'(  \     University of Texas at Austin
 =(___)= ( )
 c.." ..cc--"\_?  Internet address: .JRHarris@xxx.xxx
   c./
                     @)--;--


 *******************************************
 * Sara Armstrong, Ph.D.                    *
 * External VP, Computer-Using Educators, (CUE)  *
 * telis: saarmst@telis.org                 *
 * CORE+: saarmst@cello.gina.calstate.edu   *
 *******************************************
```

Figure 1.15:
Three examples of signature files

Interchange. It's a way of representing the characters on the keyboard and some simple formatting. In word processing, a common way to emphasize or set apart words is to **boldface** or *italicize* them. The bold and italic formatting commands aren't available on the Internet. To show emphasis online, people often set off the word or words with asterisks (*). When it's *really* important or when I'm trying to make a *strong* point, an asterisk on either side of the word says it for me.

> *When it's *really* important or when I'm trying to make a *strong* point, an asterisk on either side of the word says it for me.*

 Sometimes when you're word processing, you might capitalize all the letters in a word or words to emphasize them. Online it's better not to capitalize, because lots of capital letters are often hard to read and because some people interpret a lot of words in all capital letters as shouting.

We're not usually aware of all the clues we get from another person's face and body when we're having a conversation. We can tell if she's listening, if she's understanding what we're saying, and if our words or tone of voice is bothering her. Online we get none of those hints. If you're kidding or being sarcastic in your messages, others may not get the joke and think you're being serious. They may get offended, and you may find yourself being *flamed*, or receiving a message that is abusive or emotionally charged in some way. Flaming happens when people get upset by something that was said online. Sometimes it happens because someone you've written to takes what you said the wrong way or in a way other than what you meant. Sometimes a flame happens because a newbie asks a question or makes a comment that online users with more experience consider silly or stupid. You might want to check out whether you understood exactly what the other person was asking. It can also help to remember that everyone was a newbie at one time. Occasional flaming may be ok, but *flame wars*, or a continued exchange of abusive comments, wastes time and disk space.

One way to get information when you enter a new area of the Internet— a new conference or a new system, for example—is to check out the *FAQ*. FAQ stands for *Frequently Asked Questions*, which is a list of common questions and their answers compiled by the moderator or system operator specifically with the new user in mind.

Another important kind of netiquette has to do with how you treat what you find online. If you are doing research for a paper you are writing for school, for example, you'll want to be sure to credit the sources you use. Just as you place quotation marks around information you get from books and magazines, you'll do the same for online material you use. If you did a lot of work on a story, for example, and shared it with others, you'd probably get angry if someone else claimed that he had written it. The same thing applies to what you find while you're exploring the Internet. Someone wrote what you read, composed the music you hear, and created the visual art you can see. Treat these authors and their work with the same respect you'd like yours treated. Besides, copyright laws apply in online and offline worlds.

LINGO

Although English is the language of the Internet, you'll probably come across words or abbreviations you don't understand. Part of the fun of experiencing a new place is learning the local language, but it can get confusing. Here are some abbreviations people have come up with for online use:

BTW	by the way
BG	big grin
VBG	very big grin
LOL	laughing out loud
FOTFL	falling on the floor laughing
TTFN	ta ta for now
LMK	let me know
WDYT?	what do you think?

You get the picture. You might even develop some expressions that only you and your online friends understand.

Smileys (or *emoticons*) are little faces made with keyboard characters that convey some emotion. The classic smiley looks like this: :-) and indicates a smiling face or happiness. (If you don't get it, turn this page sideways and take a look.)

There are all kinds of smileys, and more are being created all the time. You might develop one that is your special sign, along with using the ones you like that others have made. The following list gives a few examples taken from an Internet e-mail message forwarded to me by a friend:

:-)	smiling face; happiness
:-(	frowning face; unhappiness
;-)	winking face
:-D	laughter
:-0	uh oh!
(:	left handed smiley

In the following glossary, you'll find many of the terms I've used in this book, with a brief explanation of what they mean.

GLOSSARY

ASCII	(short for American Standard Code for Information Interchange) a standard way of representing the characters on the keyboard and some simple formatting all Internet computers recognize

baud rate	the speed at which messages are transmitted on the Internet (*see* bps)
bits per second	(abbreviated as bps) *see* baud rate
Bookmark	a way to mark a site you've already visited so that you can go there quickly without having to type the site's URL. The address resides in a file on your computer. You open your Web browser, pull down the Bookmark file, and highlight the site you want. *See* hotlist.
bps	(short for bits per second) *see* baud rate
conference	an online gathering (also known as a forum or a news-group) in which any number of people can post their ideas, responses, and questions independent of time and space
dial-up connection	the phone connection you make when you subscribe to a service that provides you with a variety of online options
direct connection	the connection you make when you use a computer that is part of a network which includes expensive and specialized hardware and software that links directly to its service provider
download	bring files, pictures, graphics, or video to your computer through an online connection
external modem	a modem that attaches to your computer through a cable (*see* internal modem)
e-mail	messages that are sent electronically
emoticon	*See* smiley.
etiquette	acceptable behavior in our society (*see* netiquette)
FAQ	(short for Frequently Asked Questions) an online docu-ment that lists common questions and their answers compiled by the moderator or system operator specifi-cally with the new user in mind
flame	a message that is abusive or emotionally charged in some way
flame war	a continued exchange of abusive comments
FTP	(short for File Transfer Protocol) the tool you use to transfer a file from another computer to yours or from yours to another computer
Gopher	(1) a software tool that directly links resources between computers; (2) a small rodent that digs holes in your yard

Gopherspace	those sites on the Internet where the Gopher software tool is being used
graphical user interface	computer screens that contain text and graphics; to move around, you point and click with the mouse
gui	(short for graphical user interface and pronounced gooey) *see* graphical user interface
home page	the first screen you see when you get to a site on the World Wide Web
hotlist	another name for Bookmark—a list of sites you've been to on the World Wide Web that you've stored on your computer so that you can go directly there at any time without typing a URL
HTML	(short for hypertext markup language) the programming language used to create World Wide Web documents
hypertext link	a connection between one place and another on the World Wide Web. You can follow links by clicking on highlighted, underlined, or highlighted and underlined spots.
icons	small pictures you click on to move around in graphical systems
interface	the visual link between you and an online service; what you see on your screen when you connect, whether it's text or icons, graphics, and text
internal modem	a modem that resides inside your computer (*see* external modem)
Internet service provider	the company or organization that provides you with online access
keypal	an online penpal
link	*See* hypertext link.
log in	the process that starts your online connection; you log in when you enter your account name or number on a system
login	the word for your account name, number, or Internet address
log on	connect to the online world
modem	(a contraction of modulator/demodulator) a piece of hardware that connects your computer to the online world through a phone line
moderated conferences	conferences in which someone monitors what is being written (*see* unmoderated conferences)

netiquette	online manners (*see* etiquette)
newbie	a new user on the Internet
network	(1) a collection of computers that are connected through wiring, such as those in computer labs in some schools; (2) all the computers in the world that are connected to one another through telecommunications
posting	(1) noun: a question, comment, idea, or challenge that you type in an online conference; (2) verb: the process of typing your question, comment, idea, or challenge
PPP	(short for Point-to-Point Protocol) a high speed, powerful Internet connection
protocol	the rules online systems have agreed upon so that information can be exchanged between them
public domain	a document or application that is free of charge and that can be copied by anyone who wants it
remote	from a distance
reply	an automated way of responding to an e-mail message, offered by most e-mail programs
resources	what's available on the Internet, such as data, graphics, documents, sounds, and video
servers	powerful computers that hold information accessible on the Internet
shareware	program that is made available by its developer on a trial basis at no cost. If you like the program and plan to use it, you're obligated to register and pay the nominal amount the developer requests.
signature	a short identification you can automatically add to all your e-mail messages through your e-mail program
SLIP	(short for Serial Line Internet Protocol) a high speed, powerful connection to the Internet (*see* PPP)
smileys	little faces (if looked at sideways) that are made with keyboard characters and convey some emotion, such as :-) (also called an emoticon)
snail mail	the mail that you send through the U.S. Postal Service
subscribe	sign up for an online service, often by paying a fee
system administrator	the person who runs or oversees the operation of an online service or network

Telnet	a tool that lets you operate another computer remotely from your computer
TCP/IP	(short for Transmission Control Protocol/Internet Protocol) standard set of rules online systems have agreed upon so that information can be exchanged between them
Unix	the basic software that still runs many Internet machines
unmoderated conferences	conferences open to all; no one supervises what is posted (*see* moderated conferences)
URL	(short for Uniform Resource Locator) the address of a place on the World Wide Web
Web browser	software, such as Netscape, Mosaic, MacWeb or WinWeb, that lets you explore the World Wide Web
World Wide Web (WWW)	the resources of the Internet available by using a Web browser, including graphics, sound, movies, and text documents

The Benefits of Travel

It's all about people, you know. Whether you're reading a story written by a new online friend, contributing to a conference about the best kinds of dogs to have for pets, or looking at dinosaur skeletons at the University of California's Museum of Paleontology home page, it's people who have put together the story, the conference, and the dinosaur bones. It's people who spent their time designing a network that allows access from anywhere in the world. It's people who maintain the services that offer myriad opportunities for exploration and enjoyment. Whether you've been online before or are about to buy your first modem and get signed up, you're part of a worldwide community. In other sections I've talked about online manners, which make being part of a community enjoyable for all. The Internet community is like no other on earth. It's the largest, the most widespread, and the most diverse. I'm absolutely *sure* you'll find interesting people, ideas, and places to explore. And the community is looking forward to your contributions as well.

Now that you know a little bit about the place you'll be visiting, the tools you'll use for your trip, and the local customs, it's time to get started. Part Two describes a number of sites that you might want to visit.

 Because the Internet changes so quickly, some sites may have changed or even disappeared by the time you try to find them. Not to worry. A number of new ones will have been created by then as well.

Traveling the Internet is about trying out new paths and possibilities. Sometimes you'll know exactly where you want to go, and that will be it. Sometimes you might start out at a familiar site and wander through intriguing addresses to places you'd never even known were there. That's the fun of it. If you take your adventuring spirit with you, you'll have a great time finding places to go, things to do, and people to meet. Happy exploring!

Part Two: The Sites

Travel "Agents"

When you decide to go on a trip but aren't exactly sure where you want to go, your travel agent can be a big help. At the agency, you'll find brochures, maps, lists of things to do, descriptions of places you can stay, and even ideas for routes you might take. The main job of the Internet sites in this section is to point you to other sites. The people who developed the information for these sites are sort of like travel agents. They've spent a lot of time on the Internet collecting the addresses of interesting places for kids. You'll have fun seeing where you end up when you start at any one of these home pages.

The main job of the Internet sites in this section is to point you to other sites.

As you're exploring sites on the Internet, you will probably come across several messages. Below are some of them and what they mean.

404 Not Found *The requested URL was not found on this server.*

Not Found *The requested object does not exist on this server. The link you followed is outdated or inaccurate, or the server has been instructed not to let you have it.*

Netscape's network connection was refused by the server. *The server may not be accepting connections or may be busy. Try connecting again later.*

Here are some things you can do when you get any of these messages. First, be sure you typed the URL exactly as it's written. Typing even one letter differently or entering a lowercase letter for an uppercase letter or vice versa can produce a frustrating "can't find it" message. If you've typed everything correctly and still get a message, the site may be busy. Try again later that day or another day. If you still can't connect, the site may have disappeared, or you may have an incorrect address. You could always try searching for the site (see the Tools *section of this book for some ideas). At any rate, don't give up! It's probably not you. It's just the dynamic nature of the Internet.*

Uncle Bob's Kids' Page

http://gagme.wwa.com/oba/kidsi.html/

An experienced Web cruiser and home-page designer, (Uncle) Bob Allison has put together a wonderful collage of Web sites for kids. Divided into seven sections, it includes links to places as diverse as <u>Sega</u>, <u>Pet Pages</u>, <u>Mountain Biking</u>, <u>NASA</u>, and the <u>Muppets</u>. The collection covers a lot of topics of interest to us all, including links to other lists of lists. Because each site named is also a hypertext link, you can go immediately to whatever sounds interesting, and you can return just as quickly for a look at another place. (See Figure 2.1.)

Figure 2.1:
Uncle Bob's Kids' Page
first screen

A feature of most Web browsers is something called Bookmarks. *You can usually find Bookmarks on a pull-down menu. When you select Bookmark, you can easily add a site you like to a list that stays on your hard drive. For example, if you decide that Uncle Bob's Kids' Page is something you'll visit a number of times, add it to your Bookmark list. Then, the next time you want to go there, instead of having to find and type the site's address, simply*

pull down your Bookmark menu, and highlight Uncle Bob's entry. You'll quickly be connected to Uncle Bob's Kids' Page.

Mikie's "For Kids Only" Net Page

http://oeonline.coml/~mrenick/kids.html

Especially selected for you, here are about 20 places you might be interested in going on the Internet, including a couple of online magazines, links to other lists for kids, and links to places where you can share your work. You'll also find the Lion King, the Muppets, the Simpsons, and the Starwars Home Page.

Children's Page

http://www.comlab.ox.ac.uk/oucl/users/jonathan.bowen/children.html

Alice (age nine) and Emma (age six) Bowen have their own home page, created by their father, Jonathan. Both girls offer stories and jokes as well as a number of paths to a wondrous array of other Internet resources for kids. There are links to museums for children, games, families' home pages, and other children's home pages, including that of Isaac Dennis Bowen, born May 15, 1995.

KID List

http://www.clark.net/pub/journalism/kid.html

KID, which stands for Kids' Internet Delight, was developed by John Makulowich in Germantown, Maryland, for kids and parents. He has 50 sites for you to check out, some of which you'll find in other sections of this book. Some of these will probably be new to you. For example, you can connect to Awesome Lists, Catch a Cold Virus on the Web, Games Domain, RoboColt, and Youth Consumer's Database.

Hotlist: Kids Did This!!

http://sln.fi.edu/tfi/hotlists/kids.html

You can choose from several topics: science, art, history, mathematics, language arts, school newspapers, and miscellaneous. After you select one, for example, history, you'll see another list. From there, you'll get to a report, pictures, or a project. You'll find a castle report (see Figure 2.2) and a project that's in progress, in which Brandon Gibson and Karl Burton are taking pictures of cars and putting them up. A nice-looking Porsche is already there.

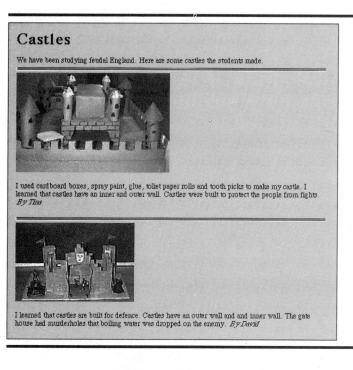

Castles

We have been studying feudal England. Here are some castles the students made.

I used cardboard boxes, spray paint, glue, toilet paper rolls and tooth picks to make my castle. I learned that castles have an inner and outer wall. Castles were built to protect the people from fights. *By Tim*

I learned that castles are built for defence. Castles have an outer wall and and inner wall. The gate house had murderholes that boiling water was dropped on the enemy. *By David*

Figure 2.2:
A picture from the castle report on the Hotlist: Kids Did This!! home page

The Children's Page

http://www.pd.astro.it/forms/dearlife.shtml

The Internet is truly a worldwide connection. This page comes from Padova, Italy, which is in the Venetian region, about 25 kilometers from Venice. You'll find familiar sites, as well as messages (in Italian, with some summaries in English) from Venetian kids to a United Nations special meeting. From here you can connect to a site that will give you the history of Sardinia and to another that reaches the Museo Archeologico di Caligari (Caligari's Museum of Archeology). Apparently Italian students are also interested in dinosaurs and NASA pictures, because those sites are listed. You'll also find information about skateboarding and soccer (the Italian version of soccer and others).

Kids on Campus

http://www.tc.cornell.edu:80/Kids.on.Campus/WWWDemo/

At this well-designed and bountiful site, you'll find all kinds of connections to places on the Internet that are of interest to kids or that involve kids in doing things. There are several general categories, including Science, The Arts and the World Around Us, Things to Try, and Playtime. There are links to such intriguing places as <u>Cute Number Facts</u> (you can learn about the number 13 or the number 7), natural disasters (volcanoes, earthquakes, and tornadoes), the Smithsonian Gem and Mineral Collection, and even a link to a Braille page. The Kids on Campus page is one you'll probably want to add to your Bookmarks list so that you can get to it easily.

*You can learn Braille at the General Braille Information home page (*http://www.disserv.stu.umn.edu/AltForm/brl-guide.html*). After reading a brief intro-duction to the Braille system, you can teach yourself the letters in Braille at the Interactive Braille Guide.*

Interesting Places for Kids

http://www.crc.ricoh.com/people/steve/kids.html

Steven Savitzky set up this page for his nine-year-old daughter, Katy. You'll find lots of sites listed in several categories, including Art and Literature, Museums and Other Exhibits, Other Places To Go and Things To See, Arts and Crafts, Toys and Games, Movies and TV Shows, and Web Pages Set Up By (or for) Kids. There are some interesting places for parents to visit as well. You'll be able to connect easily to <u>Aunt Annie's Craft Page</u>, play Hangman, get to another list of interactive games on the Web, and explore elementary, middle, and high schools who have Web pages.

The Canadian Kids Home Page

http://www.onramp.ca/~lowens/107kids.htm

Although you'll probably find some sites you already know about, this page includes some links to sites that you may not have seen, as well as links to sites of special interest to Canadians. You'll find a link to computer camps for kids, the Origami page, and the Children's Museum at the Canadian Museum of Civilization. There's a Great Canadian Pages section and the Canadian Kids Page Archive. Because this list is updated regularly, you can see what's been on former lists—a nice feature. The Canadian Kids Page Archive contains lists from September 1994 on.

Cynthia and Winston's Family Home Page

http://www.webcom.com:80/~cynspot/

This interesting page opens with two ways to choose where you want to go. You can click on one of the pictures you find (see Figure 2.3), or you can scroll down the page and click on the hypertext links. I clicked on the pictures of Pooh, Piglet, and Christopher Robin and ended up in the kids' section. From here, you'll find choices you can make under three headings. Serious Fun includes science exhibits and museums. After School selections include some of your favorite cartoon and movie characters as well as games. In the Reading Corner, you'll find some text-only fairy tales that you can download and illustrate, such as "Ali Baba and the 40 Thieves" or "The Ugly Duckling." You'll also find links to other kids' pages.

Figure 2.3:
Cynthia and Winston's Family Home Page
main menu

A Young Person's Guide to Hot Web Spots from Ontario's Science Center

http://www.osc.on.ca/kids.html

The Ontario Science Center has some interesting exhibits and information on its home page (see its description in the *Places To Go* section of this book), but this page is focused on what kids might like to see. You'll find links to schools, fun things to do, space sites, weather information, music groups, and an intriguing site called <u>Interesting Devices Connected to the Net</u>.

SchoolNet

schoolnet.carleton.ca:419/11/K6.dir

Need some ideas for new activities? You'll find suggestions for home or school projects and discoveries at this site (see Figure 2.4). For example, in the folder called Neat Tricks You Can Do, you'll find projects you can try at home or at school, such as floating arms, your eye's "memory," or seeing a hole in your hand. There are folders on Family Math and ASCII art, as well as requests for pen pals from the United States, Canada, France, and other countries.

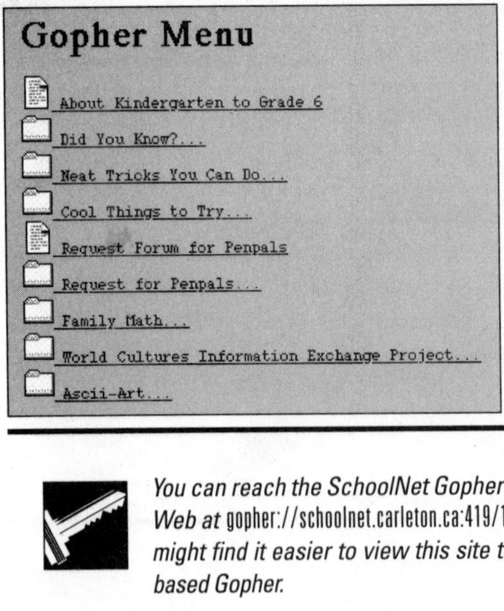

Gopher Menu

About Kindergarten to Grade 6

Did You Know?...

Neat Tricks You Can Do...

Cool Things to Try...

Request Forum for Penpals

Request for Penpals...

Family Math...

World Cultures Information Exchange Project...

Ascii-Art...

Figure 2.4:
The SchoolNet Gopher Site

You can reach the SchoolNet Gopher site directly through the World Wide Web at gopher://schoolnet.carleton.ca:419/11/K6.dir. If you have Web access, you might find it easier to view this site through your browser than as a text-based Gopher.

Berit's Best Sites for Children

http://www.cochran.com/theosite/KSites.html

Berit Erickson not only collects sites for kids on the Internet, she rates them on a 5-point scale. I'll bet you'll find something of interest no matter what you're looking for. She's got links to sites about animals, art, astronomy, dinosaurs, earth, frogs, history, science, sharks and ocean life, world travel, and more. You'll find elementary schools, links done by kids for kids, families' and kids' home pages, story connections, and just-for-fun sites. On a scale of 1 to 5, Berit's Best Sites for Children rates 5 out of 5.

The Theodore Tugboat Home Page

On several lists, you'll find a reference to the Theodore Tugboat Home Page (www.cochran.com/TT.html). Theodore is the main character in a Canadian TV series, and at his home page, you'll be able to participate in an interactive story, download a page from an online coloring book, or receive a postcard with Theodore's pictures, although to do so, you'll have to give a postal address. (We recommend you ask your parent or teacher for a business or school address you can use.) This page also includes suggestions for parents and teachers, information about the TV show, and a link to other sites for children.

Kids on the Web

www.zen.org/rendan/kids.html

Brendan Kehoe, who has been exploring the Internet for a long time, has put together a wonderful list of interesting sites. You'll find any number of places to discover, including Bert's Coloring Programs, SeaWorld, How Light Works, Kids' College (a large collection of work by third- and fourth-graders studying rocks, forestry, water, and flight), as well as Children's Books, Things for Adults, and educational sites.

The Children's Pages at WombatNet

http://www.batnet.com/wombat/children.html

Many, many resources are listed, divided into categories: animals, high schools, hobbies, libraries, magazines, museums, news, space, toys, and travel. The animal section, which includes dinosaurs, also has a link you'll probably not find very often. You can connect to a source for predicted wombat sightings in Tasmania through <u>Tasmanian Mammal Information at Parks and Wildlife Service Tasmania</u>. This site is another one with lots of places for you to explore.

Places to Go

Whether you're interested in camping, museums, art galleries, or outer space, there's an online site in this section you'll find interesting. Some sites are actual places you can locate on maps and in atlases. If you see them here first, you'll have some idea of what you might like to see or do when you actually get there. If you've already visited, you can compare your experience with what you find online. You'll also find wonderful pictures you can collect, taken from such places as outer space or inside a volcano. Let's get started!

GENERAL INFORMATION

If you like to read or create maps, learn about the places you visit, or check out the flags of the area, sites in this section offer you a lot of information. You'll also be able to connect directly to a number of other sites that have even more details.

The Perry-Castañeda Library Map Collection

http://rowan.lib.utexas.edu/Libs/PCL/Map_collection/Map_collection.html

Maps, maps, and more maps. Housed at the University of Texas at Austin, this site contains a wonderful map collection and map-related resources. You'll find maps of current interest, including Bosnia, Zaire, Gaza and West Bank, and Chechnya. The map of Zaire focuses on the area of the ebola virus outbreak. You'll also find maps of national parks, as well as country, state, and city maps. There are cartographic reference resources, FAQs, links to map-related Web sites, and general map sites, including coastline maps, earthquake-hazard maps, NASA earth-observing system maps, and a rare map collection at the University of Georgia.

The Xerox PARC Map Viewer

http://pubweb.parc.xerox.com/map/

Developed at the Xerox Palo Alto Research Center in Palo Alto, California, this
site offers visitors an opportunity to create their own maps. When you enter
the site, you'll see a map of the world (see Figure 2.5). You can start there by
zooming in on an area you'd like to explore further. You continue to have the
opportunity to zoom in or out, see rivers and/or borders, decide on the view
you'd like (<u>Elliptical</u>, <u>Rectangular</u>, <u>Sinusoidal</u>, or <u>Narrow Square</u>), or change
the database to U.S. areas only. Each time you make a choice, the map is
redrawn with your input. Of course, you can print out your final map and all
the ones that lead to it for further study.

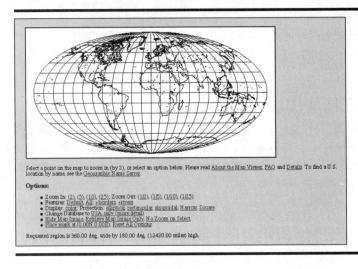

Figure 2.5:
The initial screen from
the Xerox PARC Map
Viewer

The Virtual Tourist

http://wings.buffalo.edu/world/

When you get to this site, you'll see a map of the world divided into regions:
North America, Europe, Middle East, Asia, Central America/Caribbean, Africa,
South America, Australia/Oceania. If you click on the Australia/Oceania
region, you'll see another map of this smaller area of the world. When you

click again, you'll get a hypertext listing of the Web servers that relate to the country or area. For example, if you click on Australia, you'll see a long list of related sites such as <u>Aussie Music Online</u> or <u>Australian On Line Internet Services</u>. When you click on one of those, you'll go to that site.

The Virtual Tourist II

http://wings.buffalo.edu/world/vt2

The Virtual Tourist II gets you to more specific information about countries and cities. It's described as "a map-based interface to City.Net, the Web's most extensive library of community." If you click on Australia/Oceania on the map at this site, you'll get to another map, similar to the one in the Virtual Tourist, but with clickable names, such as <u>Australia</u>, <u>Guam</u>, <u>Papua New Guinea</u>, <u>Hawaii</u>, <u>Wake</u>, and <u>Tonga</u>. If you click on one of these names, you can decide whether you want country information, culture and language, maps, or travel and tourism. Each heading lists some hypertext choices that take you to the information you want.

Planet Earth

http://white.nosc.mil/info.html

The Planet Earth Web site offers a lot of information about many topics, including countries of the world. Choose the Virtual Library from the main menu, and then select how you want to get to the specific information: via a map, via the library floor plan, or via text. If you select the library floor plan, you'll then choose the kind of information you want from a number of rooms. If you're interested in countries of the world, you'll probably choose one of the World Region rooms. From there, you can choose a region, then a country, and then decide which Internet source you want to use to get more information. Incidentally, besides having connections to a whole lot of servers on a wide range of topics, this site is a searchable database, so you can bypass all the steps I've just mentioned by typing the name of what you're looking for. You'll then get the starting point for that place, and you can take it from there.

The Avid Explorer

http://www.explore.com/

There are actual travel agents online. At this particular Web site, you'll find a lot of information about cruises. If you've thought about vacations at sea, you can find out what's happening on several cruise lines—Norwegian, Dolphin, Holland America, and Royal Caribbean— as well as what's happening on a number of tall ships (Star Clippers and Windjammer Barefoot Cruises). You can also get weather information here.

Flags of all Kinds

http://155.187.10.12/flags/flags.html

How many country flags can you find that use red, white, and blue? What are the names of some places that include animals on their flags? At this site, you can answer these and many more questions about flags. You can view a selection of national flags, flags of the U.S., and flags of the Australian Defence Force Academy, and you can read an article about the Australian flag. You can take a look at some auto racing flags, semaphore signals, and maritime flags. Perhaps you'll be inspired to design your own personal flag. Figure 2.6 shows what you'll see when you access this site.

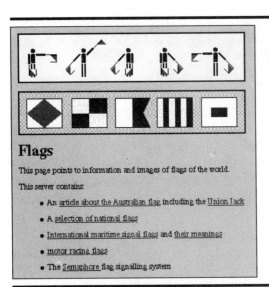

Figure 2.6:
The Flags home page provides a colorful introduction to a site with flags from many places.

The Virtual Town

http://www.cs.ucdavis.edu/virt-town/welcome.html

Now that you've traveled the world, or at least know how to, stop at the University of California, Davis' virtual town. Mayor Vik Varma has created an online town, with buildings such as you might find near your home. You can go to the public library, the business district, the university, the shopping mall, social groups, the Cinema Paradiso, the medical center, government offices, a house of worship, the job assistance building, and many more. At each site, you'll find resources and links to many other sites that reflect the place you're visiting. You might want to start with the <u>Mayoral Address</u>, or check out the <u>Getting Around</u> place, where you'll get connections to Internet guides as well as some information about the "strange lingo" used in the town.

MOUNTAINS, LAKES, AND OTHER NATURAL FORMATIONS

Television sometimes lets us travel to outdoor sights from our living rooms, and on the Internet, you can see the places you're interested in and get specific information. You can plan trips you'll take for real, or you can add to your memories of places you've been by accessing them through the online world.

The Grand Canyon

http://www.kbt.com:80/gc/

Everything you might want to know about Grand Canyon National Park, whether or not you're planning a real visit in the near future, you'll find at this Web site. You can choose to get general information, take a guided tour, get some history of the park, check on the weather, see maps and wonderful pictures, and find out other things to do and see in the area. You'll find information about back-country trails in the park (starting at the South Rim or at the North Rim), as well as trip reports from visitors and rangers. You can also get information about other attractions, including several national parks and monuments, such as <u>Zion National Park</u>, <u>Bryce Canyon National Park</u>, <u>Montezuma Castle National Monument</u>, <u>Sunset Crater National Monument</u>, <u>Navajo National Monument</u>, and <u>Natural Bridges National Monument</u>. There are also listings for <u>Lowell Observatory</u>, <u>Meteor Crater</u>, and the towns of

Sedona, Oak Creek Canyon, and Jerome. This is a wonderful site. Check it out!

John Carroll, who has completed more than 60 hikes in the Grand Canyon, presents pictures and descriptions of his adventures on his home page. The address is http://lorien.sdsu.edu:80/~carroll/.

The Sedona, Arizona, home page (http://www.sedona.net/sedona.html) is probably unlike any other town's home page that you'll run across. The beautiful red rock area is famous for arts and crafts and New Age harmonic convergence sites. On this home page, you'll find a calendar of events and information on such topics as alternative health, art and culture, bed and breakfasts, fun activities, golf courses, hotels and motels, memorabilia, reservations, resorts, restaurants, self-discovery, shopping, tours, and videos.

Great Outdoor Recreation Pages (GORP)

http://www.gorp.com/default.htm

If GORP makes you think of that snack made of nuts, raisins, sunflower seeds, and chocolate bits that you take on hikes, you're on the right track. This Web site offers a huge number of links to sites, resources, and information concerning outdoor activities. You'll find links such as Attractions, Activities, Locations, Books/Maps, Trips/Educational Opportunities, Gear, Newsstand, Food, Stay Healthy While You Travel, Travel Resources, Clubs, Associations, Nonprofit Groups, and Volunteer Opportunities. When you click on Trips/Educational Opportunities, you can get information on such diverse adventures as Above the Clouds Trekking, Himalayan Travel/World Adventure, Alaska Discovery, Geostar Travel, Colorado Outdoor Education Center, Fly Fishing Guides, and Ouzel Expeditions, Inc. You'll also find U.S. national parks organized by state, with contact information and descriptions. For example, did you know that there are two national forests in Arkansas? When you click on a state name, you'll get contact information, as well as other important tips, such as what to do with pets and regulations regarding sanitation, fires, and camping.

Travel information outside the U.S. is included for Africa, Antarctica, Asia, Australia, Canada, Central America, Europe, Mexico, New Zealand, and South America at the Locations link.

The Niagara FallsCam Home Page

http://FallsCam.niagara.com/

At this site, you'll find lots of information about Niagara Falls and the surrounding area, including Hot Spots in Niagara, Really Useful Places, and the Seaway Mall. But the main attraction is the FallsCam, which is described as "a video camera mounted on the top of the Sheraton Fallsview hotel overlooking the majestic Niagara Falls [which] provides Internet surfers a chance to access a live 10 second MPEG video of the BIG ONE itself." You'll be asked to sign the guest book with your e-mail address, which results in a greeting from FallsCam and a welcome to the site. (See Figure 2.7 for a spectacular view of Niagara Falls.)

Figure 2.7:
Niagara Falls from the FallsCam

A Guide to Stone Mountain

http://www.gatech.edu/3020/stone/MAIN.HTM

If you're planning a visit to the Atlanta, Georgia, area, you might want to take a look at Stone Mountain while you're there. Before you go, you can learn something about the real place by visiting the Internet site. You can get general information and find out about the history of the mountain, as well as checking on special events and major attractions in the area. The archery event will be held here during the 1996 Olympics, so if you're unable to attend, you can learn something about the site from wherever your home is. The huge carving on the mountain is something you won't want to miss.

CONTINENTS, COUNTRIES, STATES, AND CITIES

Wherever you live, you're probably interested in other places. From these and other sites, you can join other travelers and learn about how and where people live all over the world.

Native Web

http://ukanaix.cc.ukans.edu/~marc/native_main.html

At this site, you'll find a remarkable amount of information, organized into sections such as geographic regions, nations/peoples, literature, language, journals, organizations, and bibliographies. The rich literature section includes famous documents, such as the <u>Apology to the Aboriginal Peoples of Canada</u>, the <u>Declaration of a Global Ethic</u>, the <u>Iroquois Constitution</u>, and texts of native and historic speeches. You'll also find Mother Earth prayers, writings of Native youth, and wonderful stories. The stories are categorized as well, including myths and legends, fables of the Maya, grandfather stories, and all kinds of animal stories (bear, coyote, deer, eagle, fox, jaguar, rabbit, raven, and wolf). If you choose coyote stories, you'll find links to such tales as <u>Coyote Kills a Giant</u> (a Navajo story) and two Mayan fables: <u>The Rabbit and the Coyote</u> and <u>The Hen</u>. Although I've mostly mentioned North American information, you'll find information and links to peoples of Africa, Asia, Europe, and Oceania. (See Figure 2.8 for a glimpse of the home page.)

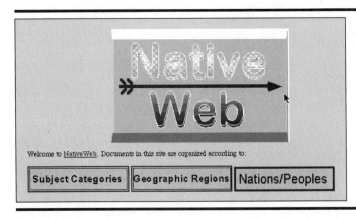

Figure 2.8:
Native Web opens with several interesting choices.

Native Events Calendar

http://www.dorsai.org/~smc/native/evntmain.html

At this site, you'll find listings and descriptions of Native events in the U.S., Canada, Mexico, and Australia. Through the United States link, you'll find powwows and conferences, organized by region and state. Another important offering at this site is Charles Phillip Whitedog's 16 Powwow Rules, which details appropriate behavior at such events. For example, Charley suggests that you listen to the master of ceremonies, not sit within the arena, and ask permission to take pictures or to tape—from the Powwow Host as well as each person you are going to photograph or record. The key is always respect, and we are encouraged to join in the celebration.

Moscow Kremlin Online Excursion

http://www.kiae.su/www/wtr/kremlin/begin.html

Enter through Red Square or Cathedral Square, where you decide on the buildings you'd like to enter. Possibilities include the Lenin Mausoleum, the Senate, the residence of the president, the Cathedral of the Annunciation, the Ivan the Great Bell Tower, Lenin's Mausoleum, and the Saviour (Spasskaya) Tower. You can also choose any or all of these places from an index. The material at this site is being put on a CD-ROM, so if you prefer, you can visit the areas offline from home as well. Perhaps you'll meet someone from Moscow at the Friends and Partners site (see the *People to Meet* section of this book). If so, you'll have a better idea of what home looks like to them.

The Jerusalem Mosaic

http://www1.huji.ac.il/jeru/jerusalem.html

The name of this city conjures fascinating images of ancient people struggling in the desert. At this very special site developed at the Hebrew University of Jerusalem, you'll have an opportunity to taste life in the city then and now. You can hear a song of Jerusalem, see Jerusalem from the sky (see Figure 2.9), enter the city through four gates that focus on different aspects of the city, as well as take a virtual tour of the city. Behind each of the four gates you'll find poetry, pictures, and information. The Faces of Jerusalem gate presents

Figure 2.9:
Jerusalem from the sky

pictures of the many peoples who have lived in the city, including Polish Jews, a Turkish soldier, and a nomad woman from Jerusalem. You'll find the title, photographer, and year in which the picture was taken. The <u>Maps of Jerusalem</u> gate shows maps drawn before the advent of printing, printed maps, topographic maps, and new maps. Through the <u>Views of Jerusalem</u> gate, you can get a general view of the city, views of the old city, and views of the new city. The <u>Paintings of Jerusalem</u> gate offers 20 pictures, including Jerusalem from Mount Olives, the Church of the Holy Sepulcher, the Kings' Tomb, and the Wailing Wall. Leave enough time to explore this fascinating site, or plan on several visits. You won't want to miss your journey to Jerusalem.

Czech Info Center

http://turnpike.net/metro/muselik/index.html

At the Czech Info Center, you'll find access to interesting information through a <u>Table of Contents</u>. You can find out about the Czech Republic, get to travel information, enter the <u>Information and Resource Center</u>, or read the <u>Slovakia-FAQ</u>. You'll see a "useful phrase" when you first enter, such as Dekuju, which means "thank you." You also have interesting opportunities such as help with finding a Czech ancestor or an E-pal. You can also download the latest copy of Netscape, as well as Czech fonts for MS-Windows and Macintosh.

The Unofficial Haitian Home Page

http://www.primenet.com/~rafreid

At this site, you'll find a great introduction to this interesting country and its culture. The <u>Culture and Arts</u> section includes Haitian paintings, restaurants, music, literature, voodoo files, and Haitian poets. In <u>Bob's Corner</u> (a special section by the page designer), you'll find an introduction to Haitian voodoo, Haitian proverbs, riddles, jokes, and folk tales. There are essays and an editorial, and plans include adding video clips, audio files, and Haitian recipes. The Haitian Web resources area includes links to the CIA Factbook on Haiti (see the entry for the CIA Home Page in the *Government Issue* section of this book), the Universal Black Pages (http://neal.ctstateu.edu/history/world_history/archives/ha), Haitian satellite pictures, and maps of Haiti.

London Information

http://www.cs.ucl.ac.uk/misc/uk/london.html

Here you'll find photographs of London and information about restaurants and pubs, hotels, entertainment, and travel. You can find out about the British Rail in the southeast, main roads into Central London (including four maps), areas of Central London, train and tube stations in Central London, and the tube system. A miscellaneous category includes information about London as a business center, classical music in London, the British Library, London estate agents, statues and street art in London, and Web servers in London. There is also information about the rest of the United Kingdom. Figure 2.10 shows one of the six shots of outside art in the city.

Figure 2.10:
A statue somewhere in London

India Online

http://IndiaOnline.com

If you love Indian food or have been fascinated with stories of trekkers in Nepal, you might want to take a look at India Online. The five major sections are <u>Business</u>, <u>Telecommunications</u>, <u>Shipping</u>, <u>Travel</u>, and <u>Food</u>. The last two offer the most interesting information. Under food, you'll find several choices. You can look at recipes for Indian food, including cuisine of Tamilnadu, Karnataka, or West Bengal, Goan cuisine, the Assam recipe archive, and Andhra-style cooking. You can get to vegetarian recipes from everywhere in the world, restaurant collections, and food FAQs. The Travel section offers a survey of travel agents who can help you make arrangements for traveling on the Indian subcontinent, an <u>India Travel Guide</u>, which includes tips for travel, things to do, places to visit, as well as a <u>Nepal Guide</u> and a <u>Sri Lanka Guide</u>.

The Beauty of India—Unity in Diversity

http://www.cs.clemson.edu/~nandu/india.html

At this site, you'll be able to get much more information about this fascinating continent. Although there are no pictures, you'll find links to such information as languages, religions, Mahatma Gandhi, the future of the subcontinent, classical music, Hindi movie songs, the economy, and much more.

Paris at Night

http://gopher.lib.utk.edu:70/Other-Internet-Resources/pictures/html-docs/flying/paris.html

Here you can visit the City of Lights at night through several pictures. You can take a look at the <u>Maine Montparnasse</u>, <u>Conciergerie</u>, <u>Eiffel Tower</u>, <u>The Invalides</u>, <u>Opera</u>, and the <u>Musée du Louvre</u>. You'll see beautiful pictures of these places and get some short descriptions of the sites. See Figure 2.11 for an example.

Le Coin Des Francophones et Autres Grenouilles

http://web.cnam.fr/fr/

Parlez-vous français? At this site, you can find out for sure! All in French, you can get information on a number of topics. You'll find <u>Education</u>, <u>Les Arts</u>,

The Eiffel Tower

Figure 2.11:
Here are two views of the Eiffel Tower at night.

Sport, Softwares, Serverus D'information France et Francophones, Politique et Société, Les média, Humour, and Autres Sites. If you check out the Education link, you can get to Des classes de Français à travers le monde—a helpful list for those of us trying to use this site!

Hmong WWW Homepage

http://www.stolaf.edu/people/cdr/hmong/index.html

This pilot project plans to "provide a central Internet collection point for resources relating to Hmong history, culture, language, and current events." (The Hmong people are native to several Southeast Asian countries.) At present, you'll find sections for Hmong history, culture, current news, research and publications, a section on education in Laos and Thailand, resources for the Hmong, Lao, Thai, and Southeast Asian peoples, and information about travel to and study in Southeast Asia. The comprehensive section on Hmong Resources on the Internet includes links to country information, Asia in general, and Laos, Burma, and Thailand. You'll find an interesting miscellaneous section that includes Hmong leisure and recreation activities, Hmong/English stacks, Hmong dance, and Between Two Worlds: The Hmong Shaman in America. A lovely collection of Hmong textiles includes samples of traditional flower cloth, as well as art produced by Hmong-Americans, including a baby blanket and other designs. See Figure 2.12 for an example of an animal pattern.

Figure 2.12:
Hmong "elephant's foot" applique design

Elephant's foot

American South Home Page

http://sunsite.unc.edu/doug_m/pages/south/south.html

This site opens with a picture of Elvis Presley and offers a variety of sources. You can take a look at *Southern Cultures* magazine, which "examines the folk, popular, and high culture of the South, emphasizing both common themes and conflict among dominant and alternative cultures in the South." At the <u>Doc Watson Multimedia Exhibit</u>, you'll learn about this folk music legend from North Carolina, who combines traditional Appalachian folk music with blues, country, gospel, and bluegrass. You can also visit the academic south and see southeastern weather maps—surface image and satellite. There are some sound files, and you can check on resources by state.

UNISA-South Africa

http://osprey.unisa.ac.za/0/docs/south-africa.html

Bordered by Namibia, Botswana, Zimbabwe, Mozambique, and Swaziland, South Africa covers the tip of Africa and includes a variety of places to visit and things to do. At this site is a map of the area (see Figure 2.13). You can click on the city you're interested in. You'll find information about <u>Capesburg</u>,

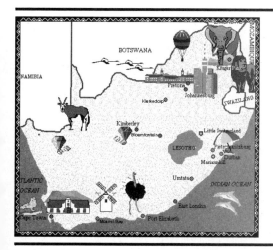

Figure 2.13:
Find your away around South Africa at this Web site.

Kimberley, Kruger National Park, Pietermaritzburg, Port Elizabeth, and Pretoria. Some facts are listed for some of the cities, and there is a direct connection to a site called CityNet, where you can look up more.

Big Island of Hawaii

http://bookweb.cwis.uci.edu:8042/Books/Moon/moon.html

At this site, you'll see an "experimental hypertext travel guide" based on J. D. Bisignani's *Big Island of Hawaii Handbook*. The intent is for you to use text, maps, photos, and audio to learn about Hawaii. Topics include land, culture, history, and recreation.

Virtual Hawaii

http://www.satlab.hawaii.edu/space/hawaii/

Information at this site is brought to you by researchers at the University of Hawaii, NASA Goddard Space Flight Center, and TerraSystems, Inc. You'll be able to find out about any new Hawaiian home pages and access earth and space science data that relate to Hawaii. You can take several virtual field trips, including those to Oahu, Kilauea Volcano, Maui, and Molokai. If you select Maui, for example, you'll be able to take a ground tour with pictures and information, or you can take an aerial tour. You can get real-time satellite data, cloud-top temperatures, sea-surface temperatures, infrared and visible full disc images from the Japanese GMS geostationary satellite, as well as real-time video frames of Manoa Valley taken every three minutes from the University of Hawaii's Manoa campus. See Hawaii as most tourists can't!

Information About Alaska

http://info.alaska.edu:70/1s/Alaska/

Alaska—the final frontier. Put together by folks at the University of Alaska, this site presents a lot of information about our 49th state. You'll find the Alaska Justice Resource Center, the Alaska Constitution, Alaska politics, Alaska public radio, Alaska's neighbors, weather, historical documents, literature, and links to other Alaska servers. You can search Alaska place names and connect to topics and links of interest about Alaska, including a section on TV's *Northern Exposure*. There's no way to see all of Alaska in a lifetime, but through this site, you'll be able to learn a lot and follow links to many sites that will add to your understanding of our largest state.

American Memory

http://rs6.loc.gov/amhome.html

Part of the Library of Congress collections, this site gives you the opportunity to select from a list of titles and topics or type of collection to research a great deal of American history. For example, you can choose early motion pictures, select Civil War photographs from the Library of Congress, or select from among the Detroit Publishing Company's 25,000 photographs of turn-of-the-century America, taken between 1880 and 1920. Figure 2.14 is an example of the results of searching the Detroit offerings. You can use an alphabetic subject listing, search the whole collection, and narrow your searches as you find the treasures in this huge collection.

MUSEUMS

From an online place that gives you information about the history of computers, to places you can actually visit, in this section you'll get a taste of online museums to explore.

Figure 2.14:
The Otis Elevating Railway, looking down,
Catskill Mountains, New York, 1902—from
the Detroit Publishing Company's collection

The Franklin Institute Science Museum

http://sln.fi.edu/tfi/welcome.html

Founded in 1824, the Franklin Institute was designed to "honor Ben Franklin and advance the usefulness of his inventions," according to the Museum's History of the Franklin Institute page. The museum is also dedicated to exploring advances in science and technology. You'll find two virtual exhibits: Benjamin Franklin: Glimpses of the Man, and The Heart: A Virtual Exploration. You'll also find some interesting hot lists and a World Wide Web primer. (See Figure 2.15 for a view of the Franklin Institute's online site.)

Figure 2.15:
The Franklin Institute
Science Museum
explores Benjamin
Franklin's contributions
and other ideas.

The Exploratorium

http://www.exploratorium.edu

The Exploratorium, at the Palace of Fine Arts in San Francisco, California, offers intriguing experiences on- and offline (see Figure 2.16). At the online site, you'll find general information about the Exploratorium, including program descriptions, events and schedules, publications listings, a digital library of exhibits, scientific images, and sounds. A highlight is a section called Ask Us. Send in a question, and if it's selected, you'll get a subscription to the Exploratorium magazine, *Exploring*. Many questions are posed online. For example, if you're in a vehicle traveling near the speed of light, what happens when you turn on the headlights? Or what's on the other side of a belly button? Or why can you see through glass? Or where does the white go when the snow melts? The Exploratorium site also has links to its FTP and Gopher servers.

Figure 2.16:
The Exploratorium's home page gets you right into a special exhibit.

The Field Museum

http://rs6000.bvis.uic.edu:80/museum/Dna_To_Dinosaurs.html

Welcome to the Field Museum of Natural History in Chicago, Illinois. Visit the Exhibits section, which includes links to <u>Life Over Time</u>, <u>Javanese Masks</u>, and <u>Bats: Masters of the Night</u>. Dinosaur afficionados will enjoy <u>Life Over Time</u>, which has sections on <u>Life Before Dinosaurs</u>, the <u>Media Page</u>, <u>Teeth, Tusks, and Tarpits</u>, and <u>Dinosaurs!</u> With pictures, text, and sounds, you'll explore fossils at the lab or in Fossil Lake. From the Media Page, you can see animations of several creatures running or eating, or you can play some interactive games that will test your knowledge of sabertooth anatomy, animal size, and extinct animals. You'll find surprises along the way, including a 100,000,000-year environmental forecast. Information about the museum, including hours and other exhibits, is also available.

The Virtual Museum of Computing

http://www.comlab.ox.ac.uk/archive/other/museums/computing.html

At this site, you'll find interesting exhibits and facts about the history of computer technology. You'll see galleries, local virtual exhibits, and corporate histories of a number of companies, including AT&T, Apple, Cray, Digital, Hewlett Packard, IBM, Intel, Sun, and Unisys. You can learn about the history of computing organizations, find out about related online museums (the <u>Eniac Virtual Museum</u>, the <u>Museum of Obsolete Computers</u>, and the <u>Museum of the Internet</u>) and online exhibits, and discover some special information, such as that found in the Women and Computer Science section (see Figure 2.17). You'll even encounter some nerd songs.

Women and Computer Science

Figure 2.17:
Women were involved with computers from the very beginning.

The United States Holocaust Memorial Museum

http://www.ushmm.org

Although this site provides information about the museum, including the hours it's open and how to get there, perhaps the heart of it is the archives and query system. Users can view information in the historic collections and archives and search for information using natural language queries. The archives contain records in various media on a range of subjects pertaining to the Holocaust and its historical context. You'll also find a guide to teaching about the Holocaust, a brief history, FAQs, an article about children in the Holocaust, and related material. (See Figure 2.18 for a view of the museum's home page.)

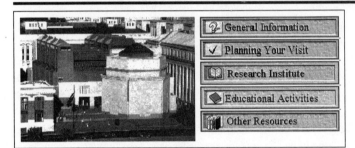

Figure 2.18:
The United States Memorial Holocaust Museum offers several choices from the main menu.

The African-American Mosaic

http://lcweb.loc.gov/exhibits/African.American/intro.html

At this fascinating site, part of the Library of Congress, you'll have access to images, text, and sound files that detail black history and culture in America. It's divided into four sections: the beginning of colonization, the beginning of abolition, the beginning of migrations, and the beginning of the WPA (Works Progress Administration), where you'll find text and pictures. This is a sampler of a much larger exhibit that is in progress and touted as "the first library-wide resource guide to the Institution's African-American collections."

There are several electronic exhibits from the Library of Congress that you might find interesting: Temple of Liberty: Building the Capitol for a New Nation, The Russian Church and Native Alaskan Cultures, and Scrolls from the Dead Sea. These resources can be found at http://lcweb.loc.gov/homepage/exhibits.html.

GOVERNMENT ISSUE

National resources are now available online, letting U.S. citizens get information we'd have to travel to Washington, DC, to find or wait until newspapers or books published it. Our First Family, including Socks, the cat, can be found in this section.

The Library of Congress World Wide Web Home Page

http://lcweb.loc.gov/homepage/lchp.html

Although most of us don't live close enough to walk into the Library of Congress every day, anyone with an Internet connection can get there easily. You can access a lot of the library's resources through its Web site (see Figure 2.19). There's information about the library itself, exhibits and events, services and publications, digital library collections, and links to other online search systems. You'll also find the POW/MIA database, other government links, and indexes to more World Wide Web services. You'll be able to connect directly to Web sites for the United States Copyright Office, the National Library Service for the Blind and Physically Handicapped (see a separate entry in this

Figure 2.19:
The Library of
Congress home page

About the Library and the World Wide Web
See what's new in July 1995 on this server, access usage statistics, and read about the Library of Congress and the World Wide Web.

Exhibits and Events
View major exhibits of the Library of Congress and read about other Library events.

Services and Publications
Read about Library services, publications, and conferences.

Digital Library Collections
Search and view items from digitized historical collections (American Memory); read about other special Americana collections held by the Library.

LC Online Systems
Search LOCIS (Library of Congress Information System) via Telnet or using a new Z39.50 fill-in form, LC MARVEL (the Library's Gopher-based Campus-Wide Information System), the POW/MIA database, and others.

Congress and Government
Search congressional information through THOMAS, and access federal and state government information.

section), the <u>American Folklife Center</u>, and the <u>Library of Congress</u> publications catalog. Even if Washington, DC, is across the country from where you live, you can take a look around electronically any time you want.

Thomas

http://thomas.loc.gov

Named for Thomas Jefferson, this site has a fascinating array of federal and state government information. You'll find information about what's happening at the moment in the House of Representatives. You can get the full text of past and present bills being considered by Congress, as well as the Congressional Record. You can see what's considered "hot legislation," indexed by topic, popular and/or short title, number/type, enacted into law, or under congressional consideration during the current week. You'll also find a paper entitled "How Our Laws Are Made," by Edward F. Willett, Jr., House Law Revision Counsel, United States House of Representatives, which spells out the process bills go through to become law in the U.S. You'll also find House and Senate e-mail directories, which you can use when you want to contact your legislators.

U.S. Bureau of the Census

http://www.census.gov

Brought to you by the U.S. Department of Commerce, the Census Bureau regularly collects information on a variety of topics. You can get information about population and housing, economy, and geography. You can visit <u>The Tiger Page</u>, a coast-to-coast digital map database, and get a statistical abstract of the U.S. (A statistical abstract gives you comparative information about population, ethnic groups, languages spoken, and other items by cities and states across the country.) Also available is a set of <u>Data Access Tools</u>, which you can use to "create custom extracts and tallies from very large data sets." These tools include <u>DataMap</u>, which lets you view profiles of states and counties; the <u>1990 Census Lookup</u>, with which you can create your own extract files from the 1990 summaries; <u>Tiger Map Server</u>, which lets you generate detailed maps; and the <u>U.S. Gazetteer</u>, which lets you search for place names throughout the database. You can also find out what's new at the Census Bureau, look at economic indicators, and read press releases.

The National Library Service for the Blind and Physically Handicapped

http://lcweb.loc.gov/nls/nls.html

The National Library makes Braille and recorded materials available free of charge to eligible borrowers through a network of cooperating libraries. So far, such libraries can be found in California, Illinois, Indiana, Michigan, Montana, Nebraska, New York, Texas, and Utah. Take a look at this site to see if there's one near you and to find out how you can borrow materials (see Figure 2.20).

Figure 2.20:
The National Library Service for the Blind and Physically Handicapped home page

The National Library Service for the Blind and Physically Handicapped

Welcome to the Library of Congress page on the National Library Service for the Blind and Physically Handicapped (NLS). NLS administers a free library program of braille and recorded materials circulated to eligible borrowers through a network of cooperating libraries.

- About the National Library Service for the Blind and Physically Handicapped
- Listen to a sample of a talking book from "Talking Books: Pioneering and Beyond (268k)"
- Bimonthly Listings and Catalogs (browse and search current and recent issues of *Talking Book Topics*, *Braille Book Review*, and annual catalogs)
- LOCIS (Search NLS Online Union Catalog and the catalog of in-process titles)

CIA Home Page

http://www.odci.gov/

At this comprehensive site, you can find out about the CIA and read CIA publications. You'll even find links to recently declassified satellite imagery. The publications section may prove the most interesting, with such resources as the World Factbook from 1994, the Factbook on Intelligence, CIA maps, and publications that have been released to the public. You can search all these publications by keyword. When you go into the World Factbook, you can click on a letter of the alphabet, such as P, where you'll find Puerto Rico, for example. You'll find the country located on a map, and you can get information about its geography, people, government, economy, communications, and defense forces. This site offers a wealth of information on a number of related topics, including information about CIA employment opportunities.

The White House

http://www.whitehouse.gov/

The times we're living in right now are very exciting. This is the first time people have been able to reach their elected officials in Washington via the Internet. The White House home page is a fine example of such access. As you can see from Figure 2.21, choices include a <u>Welcome</u>, the <u>Executive Branch</u>, <u>Government Information Online</u>, the <u>First Family</u>, and <u>Publications</u>. You can hear a message delivered by President Clinton or Vice President Gore and take three virtual tours: the White House, the Old Executive Office Building, and the First Ladies' Garden of the White House. If you visit the garden, you'll find 12 works of art selected from American art museums for this special exhibition created by Hillary Rodham Clinton. You'll also find many links to other services and information, such as speeches by the president and national documents, which really help us feel a part of our country's government services and practices.

Figure 2.21:
The White House home page

ART PLACES

Whether you're interested in visiting famous art museums of the world, online galleries that feature kids' or other artists' works, or places such as the Infinite Grid Selector that could only exist online, check out the sites in this section. Perhaps you'll be inspired to add your own work to some of them.

Camden Kid's Art Gallery

http://homer.louisville.edu:80/~mfpetr01/art_gallery/camdart.html

At this small site, you'll find the student work of the month. The teacher assigns a particular artistic device that the students must use in their pictures. When I checked, the artists were dealing with symmetry and drawing from observation and their own interests. There were drawings of butterflies (see Figure 2.22) and finches and an energy poster. You'll see a thumbnail along with the title and the artist's name. When you enlarge the picture by clicking on it, you'll be able to judge how well the artist met the challenge.

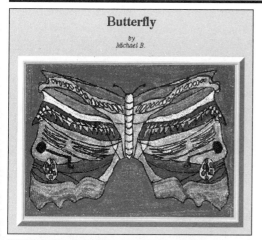

Butterfly
by
Michael B.

Figure 2.22:
A butterfly drawing illustrates the artistic concept of symmetry.

African Arts: Aesthetics and Meaning

http://www.lib.virginia.edu/dic/exhib/93.ray.aa/African.html

When you visit the Bayly Art Museum at the University of Virginia in Charlottesville, Virginia, through the Internet, you'll find some unusual objects. The introduction to this site states that African art should be "both beautiful and good, because it is intended not only to please the eye but to uphold moral values." We also find out that it's important that masks and headdresses be displayed at eye level, as if they were being worn in real life, and in such a way that you can walk around them. We still get a two-dimensional view at this site, but it's good to know what's being taken into consideration at the real site. On display you'll find headdresses, masks, sculpture, and decorated heddle pulleys (devices that hold the cords or wires in a loom).

Krannert Art Museum and Kinkead Pavilion

http://www.ncsa.uiuc.edu/General/UIUC/KrannertArtMuseum/Guide/GuideContents.html

Choose from a comprehensive index that includes sculpture, European and American painting, 20th-century art, Asian art, Medieval and Near Eastern art, decorative arts, Old-World antiquities, African art, and pre-Columbian art. You'll find pictures of many art objects, along with descriptions, which include the name of the artist, the date, the title, and donation information. You can take a guided tour or select areas to visit on your own.

Frida Kahlo

http://www.cascade.net/kahlo.html

If you've ever been curious about the painter Frida Kahlo, here is where you'll find a lot of information. Not only can you see some of her work online, but you can get information about her childhood and her difficult life, some suggested readings, and the location of an FTP site for files of her work. See Figure 2.23 for an example of this distinctive artist's work.

Frida Kahlo

Frida Kahlo was an artist, who lived in Mexico. She was one of the rare breed who achieves fame in their own lifetime. She was born on **July 6, 1907** and died on **July 13, 1954.**

Frida's art was influenced greatly by the pain she suffered after both contracting polio at age six, and by a bus accident which severely injured her.

Besides the paintings depicting her feelings of pain, and fears of death, Frida painted numerous self-portraits. These are interesting for her over-dramatization of her eyebrows and mustache, and her portrayal of her pain by adding such things as thorn necklaces, and nails to her portraits.

Leonardo da Vinci Museum

http://cellini.leonardo.net/museum/main.html

As you may have heard, Leonardo da Vinci, who lived from 1452 to 1519, is often referred to as the best example of a "Renaissance man." The Renaissance, which took place in Europe roughly between the 14th and 16th centuries, was a time of great artistic, intellectual, and literary achievement. Leonardo excelled in a number of areas, and this Web site does a good job of conveying the range of his abilities. You will be able to see examples of Leonardo's work organized into four wings. In the East Wing are examples of his oil paintings. The West Wing contains engineering and futuristic designs, which are divided into three categories: devices and machines, weapons and warfare, and flying machines. In the North Wing, you'll find reproductions of original drawings and sketches, and in the South Wing, you can learn something about the life and times of Leonardo da Vinci. This extraordinary artist, thinker, and designer was ahead of his time. Perhaps after visiting this site, you'll want to learn more about this famous, interesting man.

On the Internet, you will encounter fascinating tidbits. There is a Web site that heralds the discovery of a paleolithic painted cave at Vallon-Pont-d'Arc (Ardeche), located at http://dmf.culture.fr/culture/gvpda-en.html. *You can read the entry in French or English and see pictures of the cave, with explanations of the history and quality of this recently discovered treasure.*

Infinite Grid Selector

http://sunsite.unc.edu/otis-bin/showgrid?gif

At this fascinating site, a part of the OTIS (Operative Term Is Stimulate) Project at the University of North Carolina, the art always changes. You will see a 4x4 grid, 16 pictures in all, each picture created by a different artist. If you'd like to change what you're seeing, indicate the square and then click on Go! A randomly selected new square will appear in that position. (You can also click on Reset for an entire new grid.) And you can contribute your own square. A template and instructions for doing so are provided. This dynamic online art work is an example of computer technology put to good use. I don't believe there's any other way you could get the possibility of 86,400,000,000 pictures. See Figure 2.24 for a sample.

The Grid

Figure 2.24:
A sample from the
Infinite Grid Selector:
half a grid

The OTIS Project itself has a home page you may be interested in visiting. You'll find what are called art archives and collaborative rituals. The OTIS Project is at http://sunsite.unc.edu/otis/otis.html. *At* http://sunsite.unc.edu.otis-bin/ rndimg, *you can get an image generated randomly from the vast resources to which this site is linked.*

Art Crimes: The Writing on the Wall

http://www.gatech.edu/desoto/graf/Index.Art_Crimes.html

At this unique site, you'll find examples of graffiti art from many places—from several U.S. cities, such as Atlanta, Fresno, San Diego, Santa Cruz, Philadelphia, Boston, El Paso, Washington, DC, and Bridgeport and Danbury, Connecticut. Also represented are Prague, Vancouver, Amsterdam, Munich, Saõ Paolo, Toronto, Paris, and Marseilles, as well as Australia, Finland, and Sweden. You'll find thumbnails of the art, which can be enlarged, with some articles and critical reviews as well. This has to be the largest collection of original art available anywhere.

You can also download the graffiti art files through an FTP site (ftp.gatech.edu/ pub/desoto/graf). We are asked to remember that the artists hold the copyrights on their work, and addresses are given if we would like to contact them.

OSU Department of Dance Home Page

http://www.dance.ohio-state.edu/

Everything about dance is available through this home page from Ohio State University. You'll find dance documentation and preservation, dance history, dance and technology, musicians in dance, and other dance resources. There's information about conferences, an archive of the DANCE-TECH Listserv, as well as ballet terms, and the dancer's archive. The last named contains such interesting items as an international list of dance studios, places to dance, teachers, books, videos, dance clubs/societies, newsletters, magazines, papers, and FAQs. You can even get to the Tango server.

WWW Services Connected with Museums

http://www.comlab.ox.ac.uk/archive/other/museums.html

At this site, you are linked to selected virtual exhibitions throughout the world. Museums are organized by country, but you can also search for museums by keyword. Twenty-one countries and Vatican City are represented. The United Kingdom and the U.S. have their own sections, since the listings are extensive. For example, the UK museums are listed by geographic area as well as by type (military, naval and maritime, and railway preservation sites). As stated at this site, "The USA has the most developed set of on-line museum information of all the countries in the world." You'll also find museums with their own World Wide Web servers, museums with online information, museums that provide online information in archives, as well as museum information provided by individuals (from such places as the Museum of Flight in Seattle, Washington, and the National Knife Museum in Tennessee).

Picture Directory

http://sunsite.sut.ac.jp/multimed/pics/art/

ftp.sunet.se/pub/pictures/art

At this site you'll find examples of the works of about 65 artists, listed alphabetically by first name. The collection extends from Albrecht Durer and Berthe Morisot, through Camille Pissaro and Claude Monet, to William Blake and Zhou Jun. You'll find files of pictures by the artists, including several JPEG images of each person's work. It is indeed quite a collection, and you can look before you download if you have a Web browser. From a Web browser, the address is ftp://ftpsunet.se/pub/pictures/art.

Fractal Images and Fractal Software

http://www.uncg.edu:80/~amralph/fractals/

Fractals are patterns that repeat their own shape. They can be found in nature (take a look at some ferns), or they can be generated by computers. At this Web site, you'll find 40 fascinating art works produced by Randy D. Ralph and generated from fractal sets using Recursive Realm 6.0 shareware for DOS machines. This software was developed by Scott A. Jones of Austin Software Design and can be downloaded and used at no cost. See Figure 2.25 for an example of a fractal image found at this site.

Figure 2.25:
"A cross-section of a
Nautilus shell in
shades of blue," from
Fractal Images

Fractal images take awhile to download, but it's worth the wait if you're inter-ested in this kind of art. You'll see thumbnails of the images, which will help you decide if you want to take the time to see the full-blown image.

Electric Gallery

http://www.egallery.com/egallery/homepage.html

At this site, you will find wonderful exhibits that include paintings which are for sale and some that are held in private collections. You'll find the Haitian Art Wing, the Southwest Art Wing, the Amazon Project, the Jazz and Blues Wing, the Folk Art Wing, the Contemporary Art Wing, and Journeys with Adrian Wong Shue. You can take a walking tour of each wing or select from the list of painters. You'll see information about each artist, and you can choose to enlarge the thumbnails to fill the screen. You may be especially interested in the Amazon Project, which "features the Usko-Ayar Amazonian School of Painting, devoted to the rescue and preservation of the knowledge and traditions of the indigenous people of the Peruvian Amazon." The artists, ages 8 to 24, "document myths and traditional knowledge of the Amazonian jungle people" through their art.

The WebLouvre

http://www.emf.net/louvre/

By opening your Web browser and entering a short address, you will be suddenly transported to France, where you can select from among a wonderful array of paintings (yes, you can see the *Mona Lisa*, in color, on your computer screen). You can also look at the Medieval Art exhibit, the Famous Paintings section, special exhibitions, take a small tour of Paris, or find out all you ever wanted to know about the WebMuseum, including What's New. Perhaps most people are interested in the Famous Paintings. They are categorized by period, for example, Impressionism or French Realism. When you select a type, you can then choose from an artist index, a glossary, or a themes index. You'll be able to see the painting you've chosen, for example, *Les Glaneuses* (1857), by Jean-François Millet, an example of French Realism (see Figure 2.26).

You can also get a description of the artist as well as more information about the painting. You might also enjoy some other options, one of which is a tour of the Catacombs of Paris.

Figure 2.26:
Les Glaneuses (1857),
by Jean-François
Millet, from the
WebLouvre

ANIMALS AND PLANTS

You can find plants and animals at public zoos and gardens, but online you might find them in other interesting places as well. Whole sites are dedicated to your favorite pet or to the intriguing mystery of how an ocean-going whale could find its way far inland. The following places will get you started on your Internet collection of sites about flora and fauna.

Seneca Zoo Park

http://www.eznet.net/rochester/todo/sights/zoo/zoo.html

Visit the Seneca Zoo Park in Rochester, New York, without ever leaving home. You can get information about the zoo, find out about planned events, or go right to the animals, such as a <u>California Sea Lion</u>, a <u>Siberian Tiger</u>, or a <u>South African Bush Elephant</u>. Not only will you see a picture of the animal, but you can get a lot of interesting information, such as its scientific classification, habitat, adaptations, diet, growth, and behavior. (See Figure 2.27 for the Seneca Zoo Park home page.)

Figure 2.27:
The Seneca Zoo Park provides on- and offline experiences for zoo lovers.

Zoo Atlanta

http://www.gatech.edu/3020/zoo/image-map.html

From the map you'll see, you can decide to visit the <u>World of Reptiles</u>, <u>Bears</u>, <u>Tiger Forest</u>, <u>African Jungle</u>, <u>Apes</u>, <u>Exotic Birds</u>, <u>Sea Lions</u>, <u>OK to Touch Corral</u>, or the <u>Wildlife Theater</u>. You can get lists of animals in the zoo, find out about daily activities (such as times for the elephant shows and gorilla feedings), connect to other zoo pages, see more animal pictures, or hear animal sounds. Do you know what a kookaburra sounds like?

Sea World/Busch Gardens

http://www.bev.net/education/SeaWorld/homepage.html

First, you'll be greeted by a picture of Shamu, the whale—a special feature of this real-life site—leaping from the water. Although this Web site relates directly to a vacation site, you might be surprised at the amount of interesting information available. For example, you can find out about setting up aquariums as a hobby, get information about Sea World and Busch Gardens, check out Shamu TV: Sea World and Busch Gardens Video Classroom, or search the Animal Database. In the database, you'll find extensive information about 12 animals, including polar bears, manatees, coral snakes, and killer whales. There's a section called Animal Bytes, which provides short, interesting tidbits of information about 25 animals. For example, did you know that vampire bats have fewer teeth than any other bat because they do not have to chew their food? You can also take an Animal Information Quiz. If you answer the questions correctly, you'll get a free animal information booklet.

Australia National Botanic Gardens

http://155.187.10.12/

Birds, frogs, flowers, and other flora and fauna can be found at this scientific site, which is Sponsored by the Centre for Plant Biodiversity Research and the Australian National Botanic Gardens in Canberra. Here you can learn about what both groups do, as well as access a large collection of their research. You'll also find connections to other agencies and projects, including the Australian Biological Resources Study, the Australian Nature Conservation Agency Libraries, and the 1995 Australian Science Festival. There are links to other environmental and biodiversity services, as well as botanical, horticultural, and photographic databases. You can also find out about what's flowering this week.

NetVet Veterinary Resources Home Page

http://netvet.wustl.edu/

Dr. Ken Boschert, a veterinarian, has put together a wonderful resource for animal lovers. He has spent years collecting sites that relate to animals and has organized them in clear, interesting ways. One extensive resource is the

Electronic Zoo. Here you can get to all kinds of resources concerning or related to your favorite animal. You'll find FTP sites, Gophers, Web sites, Telnet sites, and others, which Dr. Boschert put together in two categories: sites of interest to regular folks and those of interest to veterinarians. Another large area, Animal Resources (see Figure 2.28), is categorized by animal: amphibians, birds, cats, cows, dogs, exotics, ferrets, fish, horses, invertebrates, marine mammals, pigs, primates, rabbits, reptiles, rodents, sheep/goats, images, fictional, and miscellaneous. Each screen includes a wonderful animal picture. You'll notice that "images" is one of the options available through Animal Resources, and a huge number of images is linked through such categories as dog, fish, iguana, insect drawings, Middle Eastern bird images, rabbit pictures, underwater pictures, lemur, dolphin pictures, and the Alaska Department of Fish and Game Virtual Gallery. This wonderfully illustrated and designed site has links to more animal pictures and animal information than any other site I've found on the Internet.

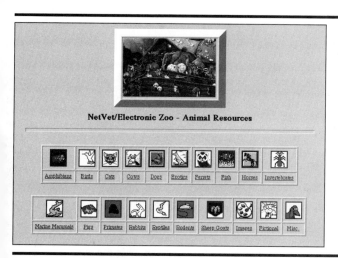

NetVet/Electronic Zoo - Animal Resources

Figure 2.28:
Through the Electronic Zoo or Animal Resources pages at the NetVet Veterinary Resources Home Page, you can find out just about anything you want to know about our world's animals.

Dogs WWW Page

http://www.sdsmt.edu/other/dogs/dogs.html

If you're a dog lover, this is the site for you. You can learn about a number of breeds of dogs, take a look at the FAQs, or find a list of 18 questions you should ask a breeder before you purchase a puppy. You'll also find links to other dog Web sites.

Cairn Terrier Home Page

http://winnie.acsu.buffalo.edu/terrier/terrier.html

Whether the Cairn Terrier is your favorite breed of dog or whether you like other terriers or whether you like another breed of dog, you'll enjoy this Web site. You'll find Cairn Terrier pictures and FAQs, as well as pictures of other terriers, including Airedales, Jack Russell Terriers (Frasier's dad's dog on the TV show *Frasier*), and Soft Coated Wheaten Terriers. You'll also find Fun Links, which includes Blue Dog Can Count! (see Figure 2.29). In this section, you enter the number you want Blue Dog to count, and he'll bark it for you.

Figure 2.29:
Blue Dog counts to 7.

(copyright 1992 George Rodrigue)

Fill in the formula below, and Blue Dog will bark the result.

| 4 | + ▼ | 3 |

Go Blue Go

Salmon Information Via the Internet

http://kingfish.ssp.nmfs.gov/salmon/salmonhtml

At this site, you'll find a listing of documents concerning salmon and salmon-related information. You can get Fish Facts, Salmon Facts, and More Salmon Facts from the Woods Hole Oceanographic Institute. You'll find the West Coast Salmon Home Page and General West Coast Salmon Information. You can even order salmon from Iceland. You might want to take a look at Riverdale School's Salmon Page and at The Salmon Project at Captain Strong Elementary School. Both can be found in the *People to Meet* section of this book.

Shark Images from Douglas J. Long

http://ucmp1.berkeley.edu/Doug/shark.html

The shark is alive and swimming in our world's oceans, but because sharks have existed for more than 400 million years, their study can fall to paleontologists such as Doug Long. At this site, you'll find 14 great photos he took as part of his research. Because they're original work, you can look at them but not reproduce them without his permission. You'll find links to other interesting places and topics such as the Museum of Paleontology, Feeding Shark, Shark As It Passes By, and Scars.

Charlotte, the Vermont Whale

http://www.uvm.edu/whale/whalehome.html

Whales? In Charlotte, Vermont—150 miles inland from the nearest ocean? As stated at the site, "In 1849, while constructing the first railroad between Rutland and Burlington, Vermont, workers unearthed the bones of a mysterious animal near Charlotte. Buried nearly 10 feet below the surface in a thick blue clay, these bones were unlike those of any animal previously discovered in Vermont. After consulting with experts, the bones were identified as those of a 'beluga' or 'white' whale, an animal that inhabits arctic and subarctic marine waters in the northern hemisphere." Perhaps you've guessed what happened. If not, you can find out at this site. There is a directory of exhibits at this electronic museum. Choose from the following:

- How Did a Whale Get in Vermont?

- What Kind of Whale Was It?

- Where and How Was It Found?

- What Do We Know About the Whale?

Through pictures and text, you'll discover how the whale probably got to Charlotte. It's a great story. Check it out. (See Figure 2.30 for a view of Charlotte's site.)

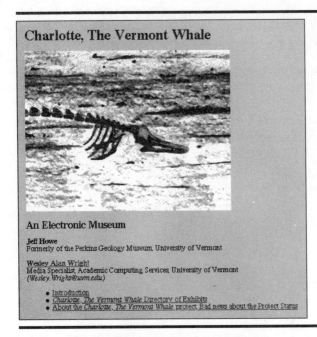

Charlotte, The Vermont Whale

An Electronic Museum

Jeff Howe
Formerly of the Perkins Geology Museum, University of Vermont

Wesley Alan Wright
Media Specialist, Academic Computing Services, University of Vermont
(Wesley.Wright@uvm.edu)

- Introduction
- _Charlotte, The Vermont Whale_ Directory of Exhibits
- About the _Charlotte, The Vermont Whale_ project. Bad news about the Project Status

Figure 2.30:
Charlotte, the Vermont
Whale home page

SPACE: THE FINAL FRONTIER

At the sites in this section, you'll find wonderful pictures taken from space, as well as loads of information about all the known objects in our solar system. You won't even need a high-powered telescope.

NASA

http://www.gsfc.nasa.gov/NASA_homepage.html

The National Aeronautical and Space Administration (NASA) may be what you think of when you consider space travel. From this home page, you'll be able to get a lot of information and visit a lot of sites. For example, you might want to choose from among the NASA hot topics list: Today at NASA, Space Shuttle Missions, How to See MIR, or Lunar Exploration. You can also learn more about Jupiter and Mars exploration by clicking on their links, or you can save their addresses and visit another time. All you ever wanted to know about NASA and what it does can be found through the sections it offers on this home page. Especially interesting are the NASA Information Sources (listed by subject: aeronautics, astronautics, chemistry and materials, engineering, geo-science, life sciences, mathematical and computer sciences, physics, social sciences, space sciences, standards, general information) and a map of the NASA centers.

You'll find the Galileo Mission to Jupiter Home Page at http://www.jpl.nasa.gov/galileo, *and the Martian Chronicle Home Page at* http://www.jpl.nasa.gov/mars.

Spacelink

http://spacelink.msfc.nasa.gov\

At this great site, you'll find an "electronic information system available for use by the entire educational community." There are text files, software, graphics, as well as science, math, and engineering and technology lesson plans. You'll find historical information related to the space program, current status reports on NASA projects, news releases, information on NASA educational programs, and NASA educational publications information. Take a look at Figure 2.31 to see the terrific home page—a wonderful picture and easy, clear clickable buttons. Behind the Spacelink Hot Topics link, you'll find shuttle missions, the actual events that led to the movie *Apollo 13*, and Passport to Knowledge: interactive electronic field trips. For example, you can find out about NASA's Kuiper Airborne Observatory (KAO), which flies observation missions 41,000 feet above the earth to study planets, stars, and galaxies with its

Figure 2.31:
Spacelink's home page

infrared telescope. There are announcements of conferences, workshops, and fairs that you might want to attend. NASA Projects links include aeronautics, human space flight, international cooperation, NASA launch vehicles, planetary probes, proposed projects, satellites, scientific research projects, space observatories, and technology transfer. NASA is involved in so many fascinating space-related projects. It's great to find its sites on the Internet. SpaceLink is one of the great ones!

Jet Propulsion Laboratory

http://www.jpl.nasa.gov

The Jet Propulsion Laboratory (JPL), one of the NASA centers, shares information and images online and gives online tours. In JPL's Image/Information archives, you can choose to browse and download images from JPL missions (GIF format), download high-resolution images (TIFF and JPEG), download raw images in a variety of file formats, and download TOPEX/Poseidon data files, which provide a global view of earth's oceans and are updated every three days. You might decide to take an online tour, such as Welcome to the Planets or Basics of Space Flight. If space is your thing, images available through NASA centers such as JPL provide exciting views of earth and the other planets and are free for the taking.

You can save graphics in several formats, for example, GIF, JPEG, and TIFF. Some operating systems read one format better than others; some formats offer better resolution or sharper pictures.

The Smithsonian National Air and Space Museum

http://ceps.nasm.edu:2020/NASMpage.html

Among the several choices at this site, you'll find a map of the museum, which you can click on to go where you want. Visit such exhibits as the Einstein Planetarium, Pioneers of Flight, Exploring the Planets, World War I, World War II Aviation, Apollo to the Moon, Flight and the Arts, Pioneers of Flight Rocketry and Space Flight, Lunar Exploration Vehicles, Golden Age of Flight, Air Transportation, Milestones of Flight, Early Flight, Jet Aviation, and Looking at the Earth. You can see pictures of some actual airplanes that are on display at the museum, including the Boeing F4B-F (see Figure 2.32).

Figure 2.32:
At the Smithsonian National Air and Space Museum, you'll be able to see actual air planes, such as this Boeing F4B-F.

You'll also be able to look at space shuttle photographs and connect to other related online resources, such as NASA Services and Hubble Space Telescope Public Pictures.

You can go directly to the Hubble Space Telescope Pictures site by typing http://www.stsci.edu/EPA/Pictures.html. *A couple of other sites of interest are the Space Shuttle Earth Observing Photography Telnet site (telnet to* sseop.jsc.nasa.gov *and log in with the user name PHOTOS) and another Web site, the United States Geological Survey "Browse the Solar System" exhibit at* http://flgsvr.wr.usgs.gov/wall/wall.html.

NASDA Gopher

gopher.tksc.nasda.go.jp/

Those interested in current Japanese space utilization programs, activities, and updated summaries of space experiments will want to visit this site. Folders include a slide show, a mission experiment, image file and loop, NASDA news updated, schedule and calendar, and two Telnet sites under testing.

Northern Lights Planetarium

http://www.uit.no/npt/homepage-npt.en.html

If you've ever been curious about those dancing lights that can be seen in the sky at northern latitudes, you might enjoy taking a look at this site. The Northern Lights Planetarium, situated in Norway, offers a lot of information through this Web site (see Figure 2.33). You can learn about the planetarium itself, including its history, technical installations, and related organizations. You can find out more about the phenomenon of the Northern Lights, or Aurora Borealis. There is information regarding the physics of the Northern Lights, a list of books that discuss the Northern Lights, and a picture collection. (This site is under construction; there is one picture at present, but more will be added soon.) The text introduction to the planetarium exhibit, Arctic Lights, is available at this site in Norwegian, Finnish, English, German, French, Italian, Spanish, and Russian.

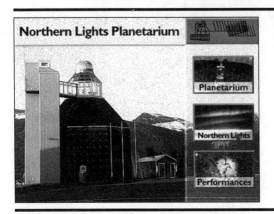

Figure 2.33:
Northern Lights Planetarium's telescope shown on its home page

Mt. Wilson Observatory

http://www.mtwilson.edu/

One of the special features of this Pasadena, California, site can be found through the Telescopes in Education link. Here you can create a star map. You are asked to fill in the date, time, and location. Some locations are preset—for example, Brisbane, Australia; Boulder, Colorado; and Lick/Santa Cruz-San Jose, California. You can establish your own location by entering latitude and longitude. You can also set optional parameters, such as whether you want constellations, meteor showers, and reference lines (equator, ecliptic, and galactic equator) included. At this site, you can also get general, tourist, and historical information, find out about scientific programs and services, and take a look at new links on the server and at the Mt. Wilson Observatory Almanac.

The Nine Planets

http://seds.lpl.arizona.edu:80/nineplanets/nineplanets/nineplanets.html

Billed as a Multimedia Tour of the Solar System, this spectacular site, constructed by Bill Arnett, includes text, pictures, sounds, and video. (See Figure 2.34 for the opening screen from this site.) From the home page, you can get an introduction and find out what's new, take an <u>Express Tour of the Ten "Best" Worlds</u>, and look at an <u>Overview of the Solar System</u>. You can learn about and see pictures of planets and their moons, comets, asteroids, meteors, and meteorites. There's a section on spacecraft and a wonderful set of appendixes. I particularly got interested in the appendix on hypothetical planets—objects that astronomers identified but which subsequently disappeared. You'll find the stories of Vulcan (Mercury's moon), Neith (Earth's second moon), the moons of Mars, the 14th moon of Jupiter, and Planet X, among others. The page opens with a quotation from the poet T. S. Eliot: "We shall not cease from exploration, and the end of all our exploring will be to arrive where we started and know the place for the first time."

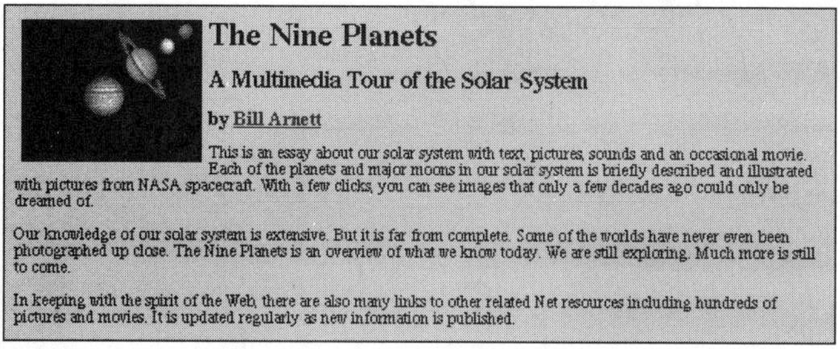

The Nine Planets

A Multimedia Tour of the Solar System

by <u>Bill Arnett</u>

This is an essay about our solar system with text, pictures, sounds and an occasional movie. Each of the planets and major moons in our solar system is briefly described and illustrated with pictures from NASA spacecraft. With a few clicks, you can see images that only a few decades ago could only be dreamed of.

Our knowledge of our solar system is extensive. But it is far from complete. Some of the worlds have never even been photographed up close. The Nine Planets is an overview of what we know today. We are still exploring. Much more is still to come.

In keeping with the spirit of the Web, there are also many links to other related Net resources including hundreds of pictures and movies. It is updated regularly as new information is published.

Figure 2.34:
The Nine Planets offers the most comprehensive gathering of information about our solar system and beyond to be found on the Internet so far.

SCIENCE STUFF

Scientists work at finding information that explains puzzles we find around us. This section offers sites that look at a few of the fascinating topics that engage young and old scientists alike: dinosaurs, weather, volcanoes, oceans, and earthquakes.

DINOSAURS

After you saw the movie *Jurassic Park*, did you want to know more about those huge beasts from long ago called dinosaurs? You can get a start on your studies through the sites listed below.

The Royal Tyrrell Museum of Paleontology

http://freenet.calgary.ab.ca/science/tyrrell/

Go on a virtual tour of the Royal Tyrrell Museum, located (really) in the Badlands of Alberta, Canada. Use the map to decide where you'd like to go first (see Figure 2.35). You'll find out a lot about fossils and dinosaurs, since many specimens have come from this area. Start with trilobytes in the Nova Room, be a paleontologist for the day, or explore the Science Hall. Other paleontological sites are listed as well. According to the home page, "Some 25 species of dinosaurs have been discovered in these badlands since 1884 when Joseph Burr Tyrrell, the museum's namesake, discovered the first Albertosaurus skull."

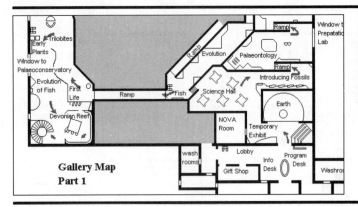

Figure 2.35: Follow the map at the Royal Tyrrell Museum of Paleontology to many interesting rooms.

Honolulu Community College Dinosaur Exhibit

http://www.hcc.hawaii.edu/dinos/dinos.1.html

Did you know that there were dinosaurs in Hawaii? You'll find a special selection of fossil replicas from the American Museum of Natural History in New York at this site. Contents include a triceratops skull, a tyrannosaurus rex head, skull, and leg, and a stegosaurus skeleton. When you click on the dinosaur's name, you go to a picture and some information. You'll also find a narrated tour of the exhibit by Rick Ziegler, history instructor, as well as links to other Internet resources.

University of California Museum of Paleontology

http://ucmp1.berkeley.edu

When you get to this famous site, you'll have several choices. You can check out the <u>Museum</u>, <u>Exhibits</u>, the <u>Subway</u>, <u>Catalogs</u>, <u>FAQ</u>, <u>What's New</u>, and more. Perhaps you'll check out the Exhibits first. You can enter through three paths: <u>Phylogeny</u> (the family tree of life), <u>Geological Time</u>, or <u>Evolutionary Thought</u>. If you select Geological Time, you'll find out some interesting facts. For example, did you know that the science of geology grew out of the miners' need to understand the geological relationships of different rock units? Through this section, you will get to a history of geologic time with text and pictures of specimens, along with an audio introduction. There are cross links between the categories and links to other wonderful exhibits (see the entry *Shark Images,* by Douglas J. Long, in the *Animals and Plants* section of this book, for example). The Subway is worth several visits. Follow paths to worldwide Internet resources on related topics from there.

WEATHER

Wonder whether you'll be able to stay dry on your hike tomorrow or when you travel to another city next week? You'll be able to track our planet's weather systems through the following sites.

The National Center for Atmospheric Research

http://www.ucar.edu/WeatherInfo.html

If meterology is your thing, this is a site you should add to your Bookmark list. You can get state, country, world, and extraterrestrial weather conditions and forecasts. An array of pictures and some video will appear at your command as well, from satellite, radar, and surface transmitters. You'll also be able to build your own custom weather map if you're running the X Window System.

Since the weather station is in Boulder, Colorado, you can also get Colorado ski reports. You can track such events as daily sunspot numbers and access the artificial satellite path predictor, Earth Viewer. You can get views of earth from space, view a map of the earth showing the day and night regions at the moment, or view the earth from the sun, the moon, the night side of the earth, above any location on the planet specified by latitude, longitude, and altitude, or from a satellite in earth orbit. Images can be generated based on a topographic map as well. (See Figure 2.36 for some views from this site.)

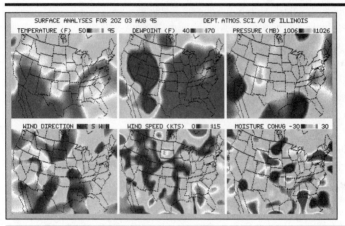

Figure 2.36: Six aspects of weather from the Department of Atmospheric Science at the University of Illinois, one of the sources for information at The National Center for Atmospheric Research

VOLCANOES

Ever want to visit a volcano up close? You'll have opportunities for seeing past and present eruptions and their aftermaths, and you can learn about what causes volcanoes when you visit the sites listed here.

VolcanoWorld Home Page

http://volcano.und.nodak.edu/

Just about everything you've ever wondered about volcanoes you'll be able to find at this site! You can get information about current and recent eruptions, images of volcanoes, an update on current volcanic activity, volcano lessons, how to become a volcanologist, and other sources of volcano information. There's a <u>Volcano Information HyperExchange</u>, which includes <u>Great</u>

<u>Eruptions</u>, the <u>Deadliest Eruptions</u>, <u>Quiet Volcanoes in the News</u>, and a <u>Volcano World Art Show</u>. Images of volcanoes from Mexico, California, Hawaii, Oregon, Alaska, Washington, Utah, Arizona, and the West Indies are available, along with links to other interesting sites. There are even drawings by children (see Figure 2.37).

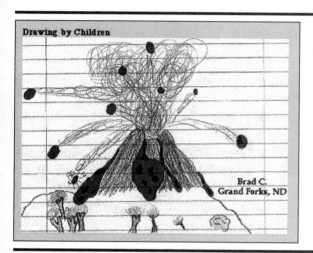

Figure 2.37:
A kid's impression of what happens when a volcano erupts

Cascades Volcano Observatory Home Page

http://vulcan.wr.usgs.gov/home.html

The Cascade Range extends through California, Oregon, and Washington and includes Mt. St. Helens. At this site, you'll find information ranging from preparing for the next eruption in the Cascades to activities marking the 15-year anniversary of Mt. St. Helens' eruption. A general slide show, links to related Web servers, project descriptions, and real-time data can be found. You can also find out about other domestic volcanoes, foreign volcanoes, and volcanic features and phenomena, as well as volcanic hazards. Continuing studies at the Cascades Volcano Observatory include geologic mapping and volcanic hazards assessment, deformation of volcanoes, volcanic emissions and global change, mass movement on and near volcanoes, sediment transport in volcanic regions, and water, snow, and ice interactions with volcanoes.

OCEANS

Did you know that your body is about 70% water? And that the earth has about that much water covering it? Earth is called "the water planet," and after checking out the following sites, you'll have a better idea why.

Ocean Planet Homepage

http://seawifs.gsfc.nasa.gov/ocean_planet.html

This site takes you to an exhibition at the Smithsonian Institution's National Museum of History. You can choose from a map of the museum floor. Enter sections called Oceans in Peril, Heroes, Reflections, Sea Store, Sea People, Ocean Science, and Immersion, among others. Each section takes you to a fascinating display with lots of good information. For example, when you select Sea People, you'll first notice a picture of a stilt fisherman near Galle, Sri Lanka. Then you can see photographs of people and artifacts and find out about the similarities among people who live near and make their living from the sea.

World Ocean Circulation Experiment

http://www.ncsa.uiuc.edu/EVL/docs/SHOWCASE/science/potter/GORE/ncar-ocean/ncar-ocean.html

This interesting site features a beautiful color video showing the variation of ocean temperature in the North Atlantic ocean over a period of one year. Run the movie, and watch the colors change depending on temperature (see Figure 2.38).

EARTHQUAKES

Whether you live in a place that is expecting The Big One or you're just curious about earthquakes, these three sites should be able to answer most of your questions.

Figure 2.38:
The World Ocean Circulation Experiment
documents temperature shifts worldwide.

World-Wide Earthquake Locator

http://www.geo.ed.ac.uk/quakes/quakes.html

At this site, the Department of Geography at the University of Edinburgh is "building an earthquake analysis system using data dynamically obtained over the Internet." You can get general information about earthquakes, find out details on recent major earthquakes such as the January 1995 trembler that hit Kobe, Japan, and check out the latest United States Geological Survey's Weekly Earthquake Report. The report includes comparison data for earthquakes, including date, time, description of location, magnitude, depth, and quality—which "refers only to the ability to be able to locate the earthquake accurately." You can also see a variety of earthquake maps, and you can zoom in on these maps to get a full set of information on the area of your choice.

Earthquake FAQs

http://www.ui.nmh.ac.uk/earthquakefaq.html

At this site, mounted by the British Geological Survey, you'll find 12 questions and their answers. They include: What is an earthquake? What is earthquake magnitude? Can earthquakes happen anywhere? What is the biggest that has ever happened? What is the difference between magnitude and intensity? What is the best way to survive an earthquake? Can earthquakes be predicted? There are also some questions that pertain specifically to earthquake activity in Great Britain. Did you know that the largest earthquake—based on magnitude—took place in Lisbon in 1755? It registered 8.7 on the Richter scale.

Hot News on Earthquakes from the U.S.G.S. in Menlo Park, CA

http://quake.wr.usgs.gov/QUAKES/HOT/hot.html

This United States Geological Survey site concentrates on current earthquake information. For example, you can find out about the May 27, 1995, 7.2 Sakhalin Island earthquake and get a new map and updates on the Kobe earthquake, now officially called the Hyougo-ken Nanbu earthquake. You can also find non-U.S.G.S. sources of information on Kobe, which include a picture collection, a map of the extent of the fire, other photos, a source of news articles and personal accounts, and a link to the Geographical Survey Institute of Japan.

*Other U.S.G.S. sites of interest include the U.S.G.S. home page (*http:// www. usgs.gov/USGSHome.html*), the U.S.G.S. Earthquake page (*http://www.usgs.gov/ network/science/earth/earthquake.html*), and the Earthquake Information site (*http://quake.wr.usgs.gov/*).*

Things to Do

In this section, you'll find things to do on- and offline. Some sites give you information about sports events or movies you can attend; others invite you to contribute your own work for others on the Internet to enjoy. Let's see if I've included your favorite hobby.

SPORTS

Spectator or participant, you'll find current scores and team information, as well as places to play or work out. Whether it's hiking, sailing, contact sports, or martial arts you're interested in, you'll find a small selection of Internet sports sites to view in this section.

ESPNET SportsZone

http://ESPNET.SportsZone.com

At this site, you'll find sports stories, sports schedules, sports results, sports chats, sports information, a question-and answer-section, and an area called ESPN Studios (see Figure 2.39). Select your favorite sport: baseball, basketball, football, hockey, golf, auto racing, tennis, boxing, or horse racing. You'll then get up-to-date information on games or events in the sport of your choice. You can also engage in special chats. When I visited the site, you could send a question to Napoleon Kaufman and read responses from Barry Bonds, Andy Benes, Artus Irbe, or Kenny Anderson. ESPN Studios offers program updates and TV listings, and you can download photographs, sound bites, and the occasional theme song ("Baseball Tonight," for example).

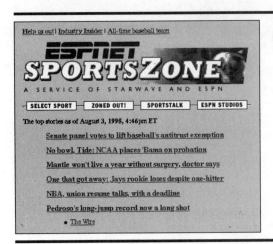

Figure 2.39:
ESPNET SportsZone's home page with links to a few of the top stories of the day

World Wide Web of Sports

http://tns-www.lcs.mit.edu/cgi-bin/sports/

Whatever sport you're interested in, you'll find something about it here, with connections to related Internet resources. There are nearly 60 sports, as well as a link to Publications/Sports Information, including Sports Illustrated, The Ultimate Sports Home Page, and Indy Car Racing Magazine. There are team sports, individual sports, dangerous sports, and sports I've never heard of. You'll find football, baseball, ice hockey, frisbee, windsurfing, rugby, golf, wrestling, ballooning, curling, fencing, footbag, korfball, martial arts, Petanque, skateboarding, tiddlywinks, triathalons, and walking. There's also rodeo, sailing, auto racing, track and field, cycling, tennis, athletic games, and volleyball—you get the picture. Check it out! Schedules, stars, connections to other sites, team line-ups—it's all here, or you can get there from here.

Young America Home Page

http://www.delphi.com:80/young-america/homeport.html

If you're interested in sailing and if you follow the America's Cup race, this is a site you'll want to visit. You'll be able to take a guided tour with Bruce Nelson, designer of the Young America home page, who talks about how he got involved in sailing and boat design. You can check weekly for new things to do and question the crew and design teams. In their online journal, you can read about the team members. You can sign on to the crew or design team, and you can build your own boat. First, you'll learn about the parts of a boat and why they're important. You'll find out about sails, hulls, and keels. When you've made your boat, based on what you've learned, you'll get comments about its speed and seaworthiness. See Figure 2.40 for your choice of positions on the crew.

Figure 2.40:
Each member of the design team and crew is vital to the success of Young America's mission.

World of Coasters

http://tmb.extern.ucsd.edu/World_of_Coasters

If you love roller coasters, this is a site for you. You can get news/rumors, reviews, statistics, a roller coaster almanac, a calendar of roller coaster events for the 1995 season, the 1994 North American Roller Coaster Census, an FAQ, and links to related sites.

Among the reviews, you'll find write-ups about real-life sites from Adventureland in Des Moines, Iowa, to Paramount's Carowinds in Charlotte, North Carolina. There are 49 reviews thus far, so your favorite coaster may be here. Perhaps the statistics are the most interesting feature at this site. They include rankings for steepest, highest, longest drop, fastest, longest circuit, oldest, and most famous for both wooden and steel coasters. You'll also learn about steel coasters with the highest looping, most inversions, highest G-forces, most trains on circuit, and the most demented shuttle loop—Wiener Looping in Flamingoland, UK. Another note: The wooden coaster found most often in the stats lists is the Mean Streak, at Cedar Point in Sandusky, Ohio.

The La Jolla Surfing Page

http://facs.scripps.edu/surf/surfing.html

If you're a water surfer as well as an Internet surfer, La Jolla may be a place where you've ridden a few waves. The online site provides an index that includes Weather/Waves/Oceanography, a link to Surfrider Online (the Surfrider Foundation home page), other surfing links, reviews, reports, FAQs, software, and a picture gallery. If you're about to throw your board into the water, you'll want to check weather conditions, and at this site you can find out a lot. You'll find not only local weather and sea surface temperatures, but Pacific/US/Global weather-related data, including satellite pictures, and Tropical Storm Tracks—updated every three hours. The picture gallery includes photographs by Kevin Connelly, David Anderson, and others, taken in La Jolla and other surfer havens such as Mexico and Tasmania.

Preston's Kayak Page

http://salk.edu/~preston/kayak/

Whitewater and flatwater kayakers might enjoy this site. They'll find FAQs, information about trips and paddle sites, paddling pictures, safety considerations, and river and ocean information. Paddle sites include clubs and groups, personal pages, outfitters, whitewater (ww) and flatwater (fw) designations for all activities and groups, and much more. Whitewater river sources include American Whitewater Affiliation, The River Pages Project, organized by country and state, and a link to GREEN: Global Rivers Environmental Education Network. You'll even find polo pages, such as the link to canoe polo in France, Australia, Finland, and Sweden.

The '96 Olympics

http://www.gatech.edu/olympics/intro.html

This site is gearing up for the Olympic Games to be held in Atlanta, Georgia, in the summer of 1996. Already you can find out where the events will take place (see Figure 2.41), get ticket information, and see a list of the participating countries. This is the place where you'll be able to get up-to-date event results during the games. A great map of the area shows the stadia and arenas constructed for this important event. Do you remember when you had to wait for the TV news or newspaper to get event results?

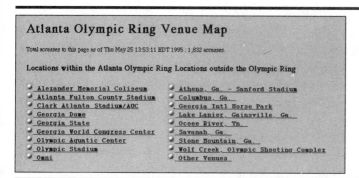

Figure 2.41:
Venues for the 1996 Olympic Games to be held in Atlanta, Georgia

The Backcountry Home Page

http://io.datasys.swri.edu/

This site is "an attempt to organize and archive the backcountry related information that is available on the Internet." If you like hiking, you'll find a lot of useful information here. The Local Pages section includes Distilled Wisdom, Fun Stuff, Gear, The Gallery, Hiking Clubs, Places of Interest, Recipes, Tips, and Weather Information. You can find out about snake bite, etiquette, Lyme disease, eco-warriors, and songs through the Distilled Wisdom section. Recipes include Backcountry Breakfast, Beef Jerky Recipe, Wake-Up Oatmeal, and Tangy Water (which is made with Kool Aid or Gatorade powder added to your water to take out the taste of the purification tablets). Whether you want bear jokes, places of interest in the U.S. or throughout the world, or pictures of the beautiful places some of the hiker/photographers have been, this is a site worth visiting.

Welcome to the CyberDojo!

http://cswww2.essex.ac.uk/Web/karate/CyberDojo/

Mounted at the University of Kansas Computer Center, this site is designed for people involved in traditional Japanese or Okinawan karate. It's a place to learn karate terminology, see a bibliography and suggested readings section, search a terminology list, get Karate Kata and Weapon Kata lists, and find out about recommended dojos around the world. You select an area of the world—Europe, North America, or Australia—and then narrow your choices. You'll see location names with either a red or a yellow box: Red indicates dojos where CyberDojo members train or teach; yellow indicates dojos that the designers recommend but don't use for training themselves. For example, Reykjavik, Iceland, has a dojo where members train or teach. (By the way, the maps in this section were generated from the Xerox PARC Map Viewer site mentioned in the *Places to Go* section.) You'll find links to other related sites, including other martial arts traditions. See Figure 2.42 for a view of the home page.

Figure 2.42:
Martial artists from around the world
contribute information to this site.

MUSIC

The ability to send and receive sound files is a special feature of the Internet. In this section, you'll also be able to learn about your favorite musicians and groups.

The Ultimate Band List

http://american.recordings.com/wwwofmusic/ubl/ubl.shtml

The name of this Web site is probably an accurate description of the site. A lot of musicians and groups are listed here, and you can find them in a number of ways. You can browse by letter from A to Z for the name of a person or a group, you can select by genre or resource, or you can view the complete lists. Six genres are included: pop/rock/alternative, metal/hard rock/industrial, country/western, jazz/blues/r & b, classical/new age/vocals, and dance/techno/rap. When you select one of these areas, you can narrow your search further by performer. When that's done, you'll get a list of all online resources where you can find out more information by the type of resource and its address. Resources include newsgroups, mailing lists, FAQs, lyrics, guitar tablatures, digitized songs, and WWW pages. You can even contribute by updating or adding information about an artist or group, and you can get instructions on how to link yourself to an existing description. Under classical/new age/vocals, I found Loreena McKennitt listed. There were some newsgroups, an FAQ, a mailing list, and her Web page. By clicking on the Web page address, I got to Loreena's home page (see Figure 2.43), where I

Maintained by Aaron McMahon (drcool@halcyon.com)

Figure 2.43:
Loreena McKennitt's home page (http://
www.halcyon.com/coolweb/loreena.html)

could find out more about her, see some pictures of her, and even hear some digitized song samples. There were also links to similar artists, including Kate Bush, The Cocteau Twins, Enya, Bjork, and Peter Gabriel.

If you look up Michael Jackson at the Ultimate Band List home page, you'll find several references, including two Web sites: The Michael Jackson Internet Fan Club Home Page, and Michael Jackson's Artist Page at Sony Music. The latter is a complex and graphically interesting set of pages that require you to register and create an on-screen identity. You'll be asked for your e-mail address so that you can receive digital updates.

Music Resources on the Internet

http://www.gnn.com/gnn/wic/music.32.html

Maintained at the Indiana University Music Library, this home page has links to every music site imaginable. The Index includes academic sites, user-maintained information, nonacademic sites, geographically local sites, artist-specific sites, and other lists and indexes. Academic sites include A Cappella WWW Links, accordions, Bulgarian Folk Music, Jazz improvisation page, Symbolic Composer, and Gopher, Telnet, and FTP sites. The User-Maintained Information links include Acid Jazz, Concert Reviews, Hip Hop Reviews, Trombone Home Page, MIDI home page, and TuneWeb. You can link to individual artists' home pages and to other information such as the Internet Music Resource Guide and a list of bands, where you'll find La Musica del Ciberspazio and Quality in Sound (a consortium of dissimilar bands).

WWW Virtual Library: Music

http://syy.oulu.fi/music.html

The WWW Virtual Library has more sites than you'll ever be able to visit on a multitude of topics. (See the write-up in the *Net Tools* section of this book.) This part of the library focuses on music and contains some large collections. You'll find Big Catalogues of Music Resources, Classical Music, Music-related FTP File Archives, Homepages of Individual Artists and Groups, Programs, Instruments, and Gadgets, and Other Interesting Links. If you're looking for a specific performer, the Homepages of Individual Artists and Groups link will get you to an alphabetic listing, which contains links to still more information

For example, at Sting's home page (http://www.ot.com/sting/), you'll find Information, Lyrics, Images, and Sounds. The Programs, Instruments, and Gadgets section has some fascinating entries, including entries for Wavestation, The Chapman Stick, guitar effects schematics, and hammered dulcimer on the World Wide Web. And if you're still unable to find what you want, there are direct links to Lycos and WebCrawler (see the *Net Tools* section of this book for descriptions). You can search the whole Internet by entering a keyword at this site.

Internet Underground Music Archive

http://www.iuma.com/

Wow! Here's the place to find "more than 500 unsigned, independent bands and artists" who want to share their music with you. You can take a guided tour of the site, check out the new arrivals, find bands by location, or choose a genre. The scroll-down list of genres is mind-boggling in itself. It includes A Cappella, children's music, folk, funk, hard rock, HipHop-Rap, Reggae-Ska, spoken word, New Age, and rhythm and blues. When you've made your selection, you'll see pictures of the person or group, something about them, audio clips, and more. You can send them e-mail, get ordering information, and find links to their home pages. The '50s-style graphics might amuse you (see Figure 2.44), but I think you'll enjoy this well-presented, exciting collection of artists.

Figure 2.44:
The Internet Underground Music Archive is a huge music resource.

Sites with Audio Clips

http://www.eecs.nwu.edu/~jmyers/other-sounds.html

When you get here, you'll find that this page includes "links to digitized sound archives on the Internet." The links are categorized into Sounds, Music, and

Voice sites. Miscellaneous sounds include animals, birds, screams, whales, bird calls, and Chua's Oscillator. Through the Music link, you can get to such sites as those maintained by music companies, Rock Around the World, Musicians on the Internet, Media Maniacs, Marching Drum Corps Sounds, Pakistani Classical Music, and Virtual Radio. When you click on Songs, you'll find an FTP repository (ftp.luth.se), that includes sites dedicated to individual musicians and groups, such as Boxing Gandhis, Elvis Presley, Flamenco, Janet Jackson, Frank Zappa, and the Zombies. You'll also get to hear some TV shows, political debates and speeches, a celebrity lecture series, and LawTalk, among others.

MULTI-MEDIA!

Movies, radio, television, and news have all found places on the Internet. In this section, you'll visit a few of the sites sharing these resources with online visitors.

Internet Movie Database

http://www.msstate.edu/Movies/

At this amazing site, you'll find "over 600,000 filmography entries, covering nearly 200,000 people," including actors, actresses, directors, writers, composers, cinematographers, editors, production designers, costume designers, producers, and sound-recording directors. You can search the database by movie title, cast/crew name(s), cast character name, genre/keyword, country of origin, filming locations, quotes, sound tracks, plot summaries, year of release, and ratings. Descriptions include color information, sound mix, country of origin, year, awards information, and production company, as well as genres and keywords, running time, and links to other parts of the database. All types of movies can be found, including blockbusters, classics, cult following, silent, bad, animated, Hollywood, and worldwide. You'll also be able to take a look at Crazy Credits, Goofs, Top 100 Films, Bottom 100 Films, Top 20 Lists, the Famous Marriages List, and Academy Awards Information. You too can vote in the weekly ballot and check today's votes. If it isn't here, it must not exist.

Paramount Pictures Online Studio

http://www.paramount.com/

You'll find several sections at this site. (See Figure 2.45 for the opening screen.) <u>Now Playing in the Paramount Theatre</u> gets you to information about several movies (*Clueless, The Indian in the Cupboard, Congo: The Movie*, and *Braveheart*, when I looked). For example, I selected The Indian in the Cupboard and could choose from adventures, previews, pictures n' stuff, and tour around and see more fun things to do in Omri's room. Another area is called <u>Paramount Television Presents</u> and includes <u>Star Trek: Voyager</u> and <u>Current TV Productions</u>. There's also <u>Paramount News</u>, which includes press releases, photo ops, and production information. Did you know that Michael Dorn, who played the Klingon Worf in *Star Trek: The Next Generation*, will be featured in *Star Trek: Deep Space Nine* soon? Read about it here, and see Michael with and without make-up.

Figure 2.45
Welcome to
Paramount Pictures
Online Studio
home page.

Bell Film Festival Infoline

http://www.bell.ca/toronto/filmfest/

At this site, you'll find what you need to know to participate in Toronto's International Film Festival (TIFF) from anywhere in the world when the festival gets underway each fall. You'll be able to preview some films, check out the program listing, and get official festival announcements. If you're going to be in Toronto during the Festival, you can order tickets and get to the city guide. If you have other questions or comments, talk to TIFF!

National Public Radio (NPR) Online

http://www.npr.org/

At this site, you'll find several selections: Breaking News, Programs, Member Stations, and Transcripts and More. Through the Programs link, you will find News and Cultural Programs. Under Science Friday, for example, you can get schedule information and visit a photo gallery, which includes the folks behind the scenes. In another area of the site, you can order program notes, tapes, and merchandise from different sites and get contact information. Using an e-mail link, you can send your ideas or your guess about the Mystery Photo. See Figure 2.46 for a view of the home page.

Figure 2.46:
NPR on the Internet? Click on the radio buttons to find out.

Public Broadcasting Service (PBS) Online

http://www.pbs.org/

Here you'll find national programming schedules for your favorite Public Broadcasting Service shows. You can check out monthly program listings, take the daily program trivia challenge, check the C-band satellite schedule, and link to home pages for PBS programs. When I click on today's date, I get scheduling for the day. A beautiful, color, clickable map shows local PBS stations across the U.S. Some program home pages you might be interested in include <u>Bill Nye the Science Guy</u>, <u>Reading Rainbow</u>, <u>Masterpiece Theatre</u>, <u>The American Experience</u>, <u>P.O.V.</u>, <u>Frontline</u>, <u>Nova</u>, <u>Zoom</u>, and <u>Where in the World Is Carmen Sandiego?</u> At the Carmen site, for example, you'll find Carmen's theme song, a home-viewer contest, and Delta's World Adventure Challenge with Carmen Sandiego (a geography essay contest). You can also sign up to get PBS Web site updates through e-mail. (See Figure 2.47 for a view of the home page.)

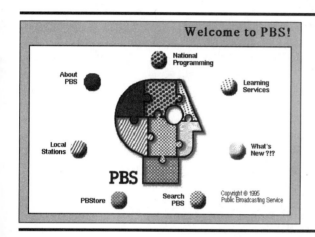

Figure 2.47:
A clickable map to get into PBS online services

Today's San Jose Mercury News

http://www.sjmercury.com/today.htm

The San Jose Mercury News, from San Jose, California, can be purchased on the newsstand. It has also joined a growing number of magazines and newspapers that are publishing on the Internet. You can get much of the paper's information online, including international, national, local, and state news, along with editorials, commentary, business, sports, living, entertainment, comics, and classified sections. A lot of the information is simply there, but to get all of it, you have to subscribe. If you already subscribe to the paper, it'll cost you another $1.00 a month to include Web service. Subscription information is included.

WCVB Channel 5

http://wcvb.com/

Boston's WCVB-TV, Channel 5, is online as well as on the air. At this site, you can tap into several categories: Net News, NewsCenter 5, Cutting Edge, Health Beat, Your Money, Asking for Trouble, and Arts and Entertainment. Net News will get you to other Web sites that "capture the spirit and flavor of New England." Through NewsCenter 5, you can take a virtual tour and find out how newscasts are produced. The 12 choices include the assignment desk, covering a story, producing a newscast, kinds of news (sports, weather, live shots), editing the story, and combining elements for broadcast. The Cutting Edge option leads to reports on the latest technology, such as CU-See-Me, painting on a computer, CD-ROM magazines, and telecommuting transcriptionists. Here's a newspaper that has begun to capture the flavor of the Internet while also maintaining print traditions.

Cornell University's CU-See-Me software, combined with some hardware, lets people at different computers see and interact in real time. You can get more information by checking in at http://cu-seeme.cornell.edu.

BOOKS, STORIES, POEMS, AND MORE

You can visit your local library or bookstore online. You can even get to the resources of the Library of Congress through the Internet. This section focuses on sites that feature wondrous tales for kids of all ages, as well as classic resources such as Shakespeare and famous quotations. Take a look!

Story Resources on the Web

http://www.cc.swarthmore.edu/~sjohnson/stories

At this very engaging site, you'll find all kinds of links to stories to read and tell. You'll find categories for Native American, Muslim, and Scottish stories. You can connect to sites that have stories for children, stories by kids, familiar folktales, and special online stories that you can have sent to you by e-mail or even add to yourself. You'll find collections of tales, other references, and an online source for stories that use puns. There's so much to discover through the connections at this site that you'll always have new stories to explore. Did you hear the one about the talented gnu in the zoo?

Internet Public Library Youth Division

http://ipl.sils.umich.edu/touth/StoryHour/

Here's a place where you can submit a story or a poem in the Put My Story on the World Wide Web contest. If yours is selected, it will be put on the Web for others to read. You can enter a selection in the Poetry division, ages 7–10 and ages 11–14, and in the Short Fiction division, ages 4–6, ages 7–10, and ages 11–14. You can also visit the story hour section (where you can read or hear books such as *Molly Whuppie* or *Do Spiders Live on the World Wide Web?*) or find out about Dr. Internet, who has some interesting science trivia, projects, and Internet sites for you to explore. In other areas, you'll find reviews of kids books written by kids, a place where you can join a listserv to talk about books, and even an Ask the Author area, where you'll find links to author pages. If you want to know more about <u>Lois Lowry</u>, <u>Jane Yolen</u>, or <u>Avi</u>, to name a few, click on the button that has that name, and you'll find something about the author. You can also send e-mail questions to the Internet Public Library or fill out an online form to ask a question. Selected questions will be answered and posted online.

Realist Wonder Society

http://www.rrnet.com/~nakamura/

This special site offers several original stories with illustrations, including The Mole and the Owl, by Charles Duffie. You'll also find <u>Screenplays and Film</u>, <u>Fables and Fairy Tales</u>, <u>Notes and Journals</u>, <u>Art and Poetry</u>, and a section for <u>Feedback and News</u>. The highlight for me was The Mole and the Owl, an (as yet) unpublished story. You will see the chapters listed. Start off in Chapter 1, The Ravens of the Brook: "He dreamt of horizons and seas, the canyons and moons, of mountains and stars. Roads and lanes appeared wherever he set his feet, the evening winds of a new season lay at his back, and the wide unknown world opened her arms, whispering, Come away." Perhaps a chapter a night, just before bed, would be fun. See Figure 2.48 for a portion of the home page.

Figure 2.48:
The Realist Wonder Society opens a door to wonderful stories.

Tales of Wonder

http://www.ece.ucdavis.edu/~darsie/tales.html

At this site, you can get right to the stories. When I checked, there were 33 folk and fairy tales from around the world. You can read tales from Russia, Siberia, China, Japan, the Middle East, Scandinavia, Scotland, and England. There are no longer any copyrights on these stories, so they can be shared. And what better place to do so than on the Internet? Most of the tales were unfamiliar to me, so finding this site was like finding a treasure chest. For example, England's section includes "The Mermaid of Zennor," and I found "The Tongue-Cut Sparrow" in Japan.

*Tales of Wonder can be found through Richard Darsie's home page (*http://www.ece.ucdavis.edu/~darsie/*), which has an amazing number of topics and links. You'll find music links, poetry links, links to cookbooks, even the Chocolate home page (*http://www.iia.org/chocolate*). See String Figures from Around the World in the* Games, Activities, and Other Entertainments *section of this book for another of Richard's specialties.*

Awards for Children's Books

http://ils.unc.edu/award/home1.html

The Newbery Award and the Caldecott Medal recognize important children's books each year. The Newbery Award is given to the author of the most distinguished American children's book, and the Caldecott Medal is given to the artist of the most distinguished American children's picture book. At this Web site, you'll see a thumbnail picture of the cover of each winner from 1985 to 1994, which becomes a bigger picture of the cover when you click on it. You can also get a bit of information about each author. The winning authors receive silver medals, and you'll be able to see the front and back of both medals, along with descriptions of them. You can learn about how the awards came into being and what the judges look for when they're considering possible winners.

In 1994, *The Giver*, by Lois Lowry, won the Newbery Award, and *Grandfather's Journey*, by Allen Say, won the Caldecott Medal. Perhaps you'll want to borrow them from the library after you read about the authors at this site.

Goosebumps!!!

http://scholastic.com:2005/public/Stine-Home.html

Are you a fan of R. L. Stine's books, especially the Goosebumps series? Here you'll find the author's home page, including a picture and biography, the transcript of Stine's 1994 live Halloween online chat, and a sample chapter from the 19th book in the series, *Deep Trouble*. You can also find out about any new features on this page by getting onto a mailing list.

Internet for Kids

http://www.sybex.com/i4kids

A companion to the book of the same name, this site includes many links, such as Netiquette, Mailing Lists, Gopher, Telnet, Netnews, FTP sites, Web sites, MUDs, and Searching. There are also activities from the book, such as Crisscrossing the Globe, Looking for Answers, The World Is a Lab, and Share Your Ideas. Each activity involves your using Internet resources as part of a project. (Sybex, Inc. is the publisher of *Internet for Kids*, as well as the book you're looking at right now!)

The Shiki Internet Haiku Salon

http://cc.matsuyama-u.ac.jp/~shiki/

The haiku form of poetry is popular in Japan. Usually with a nature theme, the poems are composed of three lines—five syllables in the first line, seven syllables in the second, and five in the third. Masuoka Shiki, born in Japan in 1867, was a poet who helped popularize this style of poetry. At this site, you can participate in a haiku contest, read some of Masuoka's poetry, learn something about why Japanese people are interested in haiku written in English, and find out how to compose and appreciate the form. You can join the mailing list and connect to other poetry-related sites. You'll even find a new form: SciFaiku. The content of these haiku (which may or may not follow the syllable count) has to do with science fiction. For example:

Asteroids collide

Without a sound . . .

We maneuver between the fragments.

You may want to try your hand at this ancient art and share your work at this site. (See Figure 2.49 for a sample page from this site.)

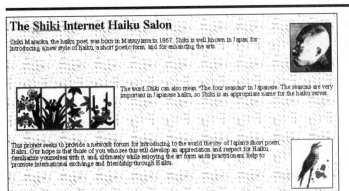

Figure 2.49:
The Shiki Internet Haiku Salon brings together people all over the world who are interested in this special kind of poetry.

The Compelete Works of William Shakespeare

http://the-tech.mit.edu/Shakespeare/works.html

It's all here. All of Shakespeare's plays and poetry, Bartlett's familiar Shakespearean quotations, FAQs, and links to other Shakespeare resources on the

Net. You can search the texts for words and get a chronological listing of the plays. When you decide on a play, you will see the Dramatis Personae (a list of the characters in the play, with brief explanations). It contains some links for words that today may have a meaning that is different from the meaning in Shakespeare's time. For example, did you know that if someone was called Sir, it didn't mean he was honored by the king or queen, but that he had earned a bachelor of arts degree from a university? After you find out about the characters in the play, you'll see the whole text of the play. Whether you are simply interested in Shakespeare, are working on a play at school, or preparing a school report, you'll find this site valuable for its insights into Shakespeare's time and the meaning behind his plays.

Bartlett's Familiar Quotations

http://www.cc.columbia.edu/acis/bartleby/bartlett/index.html

In this searchable database, you can look for words or access an alphabetic index of authors. In addition, an extensive chronological index of primary authors starts with Geoffrey Chaucer (1328–1400) and ends with Von Münch Bellinghausen (1806–71). The sources include biblical and other religious writings, as well as 14th-century to 19th-century writers and thinkers, so searching for *computer* or *technology* turns up no results. However, when you do find a word, you'll get a reference that includes the author, a partial quotation that includes the word, and the name of the work in which it occurred. You can also look up words in the Old Testament, the New Testament, the Book of Common Prayer, and Tate and Brady. Sometimes it's fun to browse; you might end up with some jewels. (See Figure 2.50 for a view of the home page.)

Figure 2.50:
Mr. Bartlett's home page

Children's Literature Web Guide

http://www.ucalgary.ca/~dkbrown/index.html

This site is amazing! Whether you want to look at some online children's stories or read-along stories, find out about children's book awards, check on recommended books, see which children's books are being made into movies, or learn more about your favorite author, the information is probably here. You'll find links to other Internet sites, including sections listing books, libraries, and cool stuff for kids. There's even information about fictional people and places, such as <u>Nancy Drew</u>, <u>Oz</u>, and <u>Winnie-the-Pooh</u>. Through this last link you can get to the <u>Pooh-FAQ</u>, find out how to play <u>Virtual Pooh-Sticks</u>, and check out the <u>Pooh Trivia Quiz</u>. It's all here!

Many of your favorite authors have their own home pages, which you'll find at the Children's Literature Web Guide site. For example, you'll find Lewis Carroll at http://ux4.cso.uiuc.edu/~jbirenba/carroll.html, *Madeleine L'Engle at* gopher.wheaton.edu/1/Wheaton_Archives/SC/findaids/sc03, *and Dr. Seuss at* http://klinzhai.iuma.com/~drseuss/seuss.

YOUR WORK

The Internet offers some special opportunities for kids to publish their work. The sites in this section invite you to participate by creating online art or by adding your own research, stories, drawings, or music to existing collections.

Kids' Space New Directory

http://www.interport.net/kids-space

This site—International Kids' Space—is a place on the Net where you can share your writing, your art, or your music. Through the <u>Story Book</u> link, you can read what other kids have written and, if you choose, submit a picture you made based on the story. You can do a similar thing through the <u>Kids' Gallery</u> link: look at a picture and write a story about it to submit. Of course, you can send in a story or a picture that will simply be added to either collection for others' responses. Artists are grouped by age, so you can find what others your age have submitted. In <u>On Air Concert</u>, you can hear sound files sent in by kids. When I looked, there was a song and music played on piano, treble recorder, trumpet, and violin. Each entry contains the name of the artist, the age of the artist, the title of the work, a link to the artist's home page or e-mail address, and the artist's country flag. At the Doctor's Help Office, you can get some technical help. At the Mail Office, you can post messages on the Bulletin Board or find pen pals from all over the world in the Pen-pal Box. Forms for all submissions are included on the site. See Figure 2.51 for a view of the home page.

Figure 2.51:
A colorful, clickable map welcomes everyone to this site.

Publishing on KidPub

http://escrime.en-garde.com:80/kidpub/

This Web site is all about kids publishing their own stories and poems. It includes a template for submitting a story; so that's easy to do. You'll find lots of kids' writings already online—nearly 200 when I looked. You can choose what you want to read. Here are some examples:

- Zack and His Worst Walk Home From School, by Ryan Converse, age 7

- Pinky, the Pig Who Loved Cheese! by Danielle Coffey, age 11

- The Deadly Game of Tag, by Joseph Marchesano, age 11

- Mark and Me, by Leanne Nguyen, age 12 (who wrote the story when she was 10)

◆   Have You Ever Tried C.P.R. on a Foot? a poem by Caitlin Grogan, age 10

You'll also find a bit about each author, along with his or her e-mail address.

Kidopedia Control Center

http://rdz.stjohns.edu/kidopedia/ControlCenter/ControlCenter.html

Here you get a chance to help build an online encyclopedia with information provided by kids only. This site is under development, and you'll find instructions about how to add articles and how to connect the site to your home page. Downloading can be slow, but it's worth the wait. You'll find alphabet letters to click on, which gets you to topics. For example, clicking on A gets you to astronomy, animals, and authors. If you click on animals, you'll get another list, including brown bear, crabs, and eels. If you click on brown bear, you'll find Olivia's offering: "Bears can't see or hear very good, but they smell great." With each submission, you'll include your name, school, e-mail address, teacher, grade, and date submitted. You can also search the entries by grade level, and soon other languages will be included. You can also find out how to start a local Kidopedia and visit others in Australia, the Netherlands, and the U.S.

ISH KidNews

http://www.umassd.edu/SpecialPrograms/ISN/KidNews.html

Here's the International Student Newswire, to which you can make submissions in a variety of areas, for example: news stories, feature stories, profile stories, how-to stories, reviews, sports stories, poetry, and fiction. Links include Kids Discussion and Cool Hangouts. Under reviews, you'll find one for *Sports Illustrated Magazine for Kids* and book, restaurant, movie, and software reviews. How-to stories include making your own bracelet and street hockey safety tips. Behind the Feature Stories link, you'll find Alaska's Iditarod Dog Sled Race, Texas' Iditarod II Cat Sled Race, Teachers with Kids in Their Own School, Girls Join Boys at Recess, Fluoride Swishing Not the Best Taste, and Recess: Good, Bad, Ugly. There are instructions on how to submit your work, and you'll even find pointers for writing your story in Kids Discussion. (See Figure 2.52 for a sample from this page.)

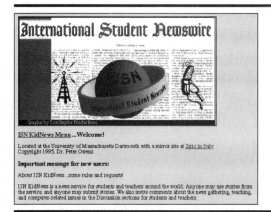

Figure 2.52:
Welcome to the International Student Newswire home page.

The Asylum's Lite-Brite

http://www.galcit.caltech.edu/~ta/lb/lb.html

Remember that game? You poke holes in a pattern, and light shines through to illuminate your picture? Here's an online version. The site has many, many pictures for you to see, done by visitors. You can contribute as well. You'll find the current featured work, you can take a Random Walk through the art collection, visit the Gallery, or jump into previous months' pictures, starting in May 1994. I visited toward the end of the month, and there were already 373 works in the gallery for that month. It's easy to do. You can work with givens—an 8x8 grid, with default colors (red, green, yellow, orange, blue, violet, and white). Or you can define the size of the grid—as many as 50 columns and 50 rows—and set your own colors. You can indicate which colors go where by clicking on boxes next to the pegs, or you can enter the letter codes in rows. You can preview your picture at any time. Advanced picture editing tools let you shift the picture up or down, and add or delete rows or columns. When you're finished, you enter the title of your work and your name, and you become one of the current month's exhibitors.

You know those pictures you have to look at by crossing your eyes and then uncrossing them until you can see what's really there? At the Weird Three Dimensional Page! (http://neoteny.eccosys.com/cyrus/rds.html), you'll find some of those random dot stereograms. At this site are several images and connections to others. See if you can make out what's "behind" the pictures.

Global Show-Tell

http://www.manymedia.com/show-tell/

Here you'll find a "virtual exhibition that lets children show off their favorite projects, possessions, accomplishments, and collections to kids (and adults) around the world." You can go to three main places from the home page: Visit the Exhibition, Other Sites of Interest, and How to Enter. The exhibition consists of links to artwork at Web and FTP sites. To participate, you send e-mail with instructions on reaching the WWW or FTP site and the filename in which your graphics reside. In the meantime, take a look at the artists already online.

CyberKids

http://www.woodwind.com/mtlake/CyberKids/CyberKids.html

At this site you'll find lots to see and do. In CyberKids Magazine, you'll find articles and stories, such as "The Battle of Fort Eagle," by Will Fowler, age 10, and "The Singing of the Cicadas, Parts I and II," by Molly Sweeney, age 13. Or, if you select CyberKids Launchpad, you'll find links to some interesting sites such as WebLouvre, The Exploratorium, Carlos' Coloring Book, and Global Show–Tell (you'll find full descriptions of all these sites in this book). Another option, CyberKids Interactive, is a place for kids to share their thoughts and ideas, what they liked, and what they disliked about CyberKids and to find *keypals* (online pen pals). You'll find kids' artwork too (see Figure 2.53 for an example). Mountain Lake Software, the developer of this page, even makes available some free fonts.

Student Artwork

http://www.cnyric.org/blissproj/blissart.html

At this site, you'll find a collection of artwork created by seventh-graders. They designed postage stamps to reflect the muse that inspired several artists. This project is part of a collaborative work to create an electronic book, In Search of the Creative Muse. You'll find interpretations of The Desert Muse of Cézanne, The Outrageous Muse of O'Keeffe (see Figure 2.54), The Pastel Muse of Monet, The Powerful Muse of Picasso, and The Violent Muse of Van Gogh. Each chapter contains two to six images, about 64 K each.

Figure 2.53:
Children's art is included in the CyberKids'
home page.

Figure 2.54:
Two students' views of Georgia O'Keeffe's muse

Interactive Drumming Experiment

http://fiat.gslis.utexas.edu/~therion/drumming.html

Perhaps you saw Out of Chaos perform at Robofest 6. The nine-member
"loose coalition of Austin, Texas based African, Middle-Eastern, and Caribbean

drummers" band has contributed some of its music to this Web site. You are encouraged to download the sound files, record yourself jamming to the music, and then upload your performance. Someone else will download yours, add to it, and upload it, and on, and on. An incredible, ever-changing, worldwide collaboration of musicians can take place right here!

CareerMosaic

http://www.careermosaic.com/

At this site, you'll find the Jobs.Offered database, which is pulled together from many Internet sites, along with other sections, including <u>Employers</u>, <u>College Connection</u>, <u>InfoCenter</u>, and <u>Special Features</u>. The <u>International Herald Tribune</u> has been added for wider job searches. Through the College Connection (found directly at http://www.careermosaic.com/cm/cm31.html), you'll find a list of employers you can click on. Each company provides an introduction to who it is and other information, such as entry-level opportunities, campus recruiting calendar, and internships. If you're starting to think about entering the job market, you might want to take a look at this site to get some idea about what's out there.

WHAT DID YOU SAY?

Language learning can be a lot of fun and is always interesting. The sites in this section get you started in some languages and offer opportunities for connecting with myriad language resources.

Human Languages Page

http://www.willamette.edu/~tjones/Language-Page.html

This page contains a long list of sites, arranged alphabetically, under the heading Languages and Literature. You'll find nearly 60 languages of the world, including the <u>Aboriginal Studies Electronic Data Archive</u>, the <u>Afrikaans</u> home page (in Afrikaans), <u>Akkadian</u> language (Babylonian and Assyrian cuneiform texts), <u>Arabic</u>, <u>Gaelic</u>, <u>Hindi</u>, <u>Yiddish</u>, <u>Vietnamese</u>, <u>Native American Languages</u>, <u>Esperanto</u>, and <u>Finnish</u>. If I haven't mentioned the language you're interested in, take a look at this site. The one you want is probably there. You'll also find multilingual resources, book/text collections, linguistics laboratories and institutions on the Net, and commercial resources.

Web Spanish Lessons

http://www.willamette.edu/~tjones/Spanish/Spanish-main.html

A fellow named Tyler Jones decided to put some time and energy into offering an online course "intended to give English speakers a beginner's knowledge of Mexican Spanish." The lessons include audio clips to aid in pronouncing new words. (Macintosh and Windows users can download sound players from a link to Tyler's FTP area.) So far, you'll find three lessons, which provide new words, pronunciation information, examples in Spanish, and occasional opportunities to test yourself. Tyler uses a form in which you can type the English or Spanish translation and then check your answers. He plans to offer additional lessons every month or two for the next 10–12 months. (See Figure 2.55 for a view of this site.)

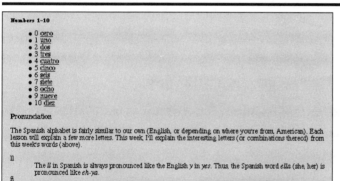

Figure 2.55:
A typical lesson at this site includes vocabulary and pronunciation information.

French Lesson Home Page

http://teleglobe.ca/~leo/french.html

Perhaps French is the language you've been wanting to learn. You can visit this site and work through Jacques Léon's lessons. There are nine so far, plus additional vocabulary, and expressions and idioms. You can work at your own rate, skip around in the lessons, or follow them sequentially (probably the better idea for beginners). You'll also find links to a French Page and some of the page author's own writings.

Web Italian Lessons Homepage

http://www.willamette.edu/~tjones/languages/Italian/Italian-lesson.html

After seeing Tyler Jones's Spanish lessons online, another Net traveler decided to follow suit and share lessons in Italian. Lucio Chiappetti has thus far created two lessons, with more to come. In Lesson 1, you'll find nouns and simple phrases, words you're likely to run into, numbers 1–10, and pronunciation information. Lesson 2 introduces colors, the numbers 11–99, verb conjugation, definite and indefinite articles, agreement and placement of adjectives, examples, and more pronunciation examples.

Travelers' Japanese with Voice

http://www.ntt.jp/japan/japanese

If you've got a visit to Japan in your future, take a look at this site. You'll find a pronunciation guide—text explanations and a recorded voice to say the sounds for you—as well as several categories of useful phrases. The Essential Expressions section includes such examples as how to say yes, no, that's right, thank you, thank you very much, excuse me, good morning, see you later, I understand, and I'm looking for someone who speaks English (Eigo no dekiru hito wa imasuka). You can find out how to say "I would like to order" or "What is this?" at a restaurant or "I am lost. Where am I on this map?" There's a link to Japanese Information, where you can find a Japanese version of the page, the national anthem, geography, cultures and customs, tourist information, sports, the government, the law, communication, and other Internet sites.

Games, Activities, and Other Entertainments 125

Sign Languages

http://www.computel.com/~mernix/deafworld/nonref/lang/lang.html

At this unique site in Lyons, France, you'll get an explanation of sign languages, including the fact that American, British, and French signs are different. You can also choose to see alphabetic pictures of French Sign Language and peruse a French Signs Database and a Finger Spelling Guide. You can get different definitions of American Sign Language and connect to a Gopher site that has a report on American Sign Language (called Ameslan) by Megan Deslippe from Michigan State University. A French Signs Database is currently under construction. (Figure 2.56 offers a look at this site.)

Figure 2.56:
People may mean different things when they talk about sign language. At this site, you can start looking at similarities and differences.

GAMES, ACTIVITIES, AND OTHER ENTERTAINMENTS

Games you can play offline often take on new dimensions when you play them on the Internet. Who would have thought you could send electronic postcards, check out the latest Dilbert cartoon, challenge yourself with math games, dissect a frog, or construct Mr. Potato Head online? These and many more engaging activities await you.

The Games Domain

http://wcl-rs.bham.ac.uk/GamesDomain

Lots and lots of game information can be found at this site. You'll find a section on Competitions, the GD Review (a new gaming magazine), Games Information, Games Programming, and Direct Download. Through Games Information, you can get to a number of Internet game resources, divided into categories such as Commercial Home Pages, the Universal Hint System, Games FAQs, Game Related FTP links, home pages, and magazines. Each section has a good number of links. For example, there are 58 FTP links, divided into IBM PC, OS/2, Amiga, Mac, X, and miscellaneous. You'll even find a category of Walkthroughs with a warning: ". . . only look if you are really stuck, and then be careful that you don't spoil the whole game."

Games Domain (Game Bytes)

http://sunsite.unc.edu/GameBytes

Not to be confused with the previous entry, this place is completely different. Game Bytes is an online newsletter in which you'll find reviews of an unbelievable number of computer games. Issues #1–21 are online. You can also see an article index in chart form, listing product titles alphabetically, with reviews, previews, tips, and issue numbers. From issue 18 on, you'll find links to the articles themselves. Game Bytes #21 includes a review of Doom 2, previews of Bio Forge, Dark Forces, Donkey Kong Country, Rise of the Triad, and VFX-1. I took a look at the review of Master of Magic. You'll find requirements, an overview, options, how to play, and comments on features. The extensive review includes thumbnails of some game screens and gives the writer's conclusions about the game. You too can be a reviewer for Game Bytes. Check out the Game Bytes Writer's Guidelines and Want to Write for Game Bytes? links to find out how.

You can get to Game Bytes issues through anonymous FTP at ftp.uml.edu.

Carlos's Coloring Book Home Page

http://robot0.ge.uiuc.edu/~carlosp/color/

Carlos has put up two kinds of coloring books for you: Simple and Expert. The difference between the two books is how the color fills in the objects. Both books let you choose a picture to color: birthday, Christmas, crown, flower, house, or snowman. Both let you choose from among 10 colors. In the Simple book, you can only put in one color at a time, but you get to see the picture change each time you add a color. In the Expert book, you click on the colors and on the spot where you want them, but you won't see them until you're done and click on "process image." Then they'll all fill in. The best part of this site is that you can download the software so that you can color in the pictures at your own house without being online. (See Figure 2.57 for an example of a shape to color from Carlos's site).

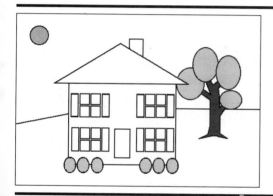

Figure 2.57:
A sample page from the Expert coloring book

This Is Mega-Mathematics!

http://www.c3.lanl.gov/~captors/mega-math/

From Los Alamos National Laboratory, Computer Research and Applications Group (which includes teachers, mathematicians, computer science and education students, elementary and high school students, school administrators, computer scientists, and parents) comes this site. It presents a variety of engaging math problems to solve. You'll find visual and text indexes to the contents. The mathematical topics include the most colorful math of all, games on graphs, untangling the mathematics of knots, algorithms and ice cream for all, machines that eat your words, welcome to the Hotel Infinity, and a usual day at Unusual School. You can also look at hints for navigating MegaMath, stories, writings from the Megamath Project, the MegaMath Glossary and Reference Section, the MegaMath Mailbox, and a section of links to related sites. Each math challenge opens to its own section and includes activities, vocabulary, background information, preparation and materials, big ideas and key concepts, evaluation, and National Council for Teachers of Mathematics tie-ins. The stories, which describe each math challenge and a solution, are illustrated and are in large type.

This site contains lots of graphics and downloads very slowly! You may want to turn off the automatic loading of graphics before you get here.

MathMagic!

http://forum.swarthmore.edu/mathmagic/

MathMagic! is designed for kids who like to work on math problems together. You'll find current and past challenges, grouped by grade level (K–3, 4–6, 7–9, and 10–12). If you decide to participate, you can register to play. You and your team will work with another to solve the challenge. When you agree on a solution, you post it for the pair of teams. You can take a look at past challenges by grade level by clicking on their links. See Figure 2.58 for an example of a 4–6 challenge.

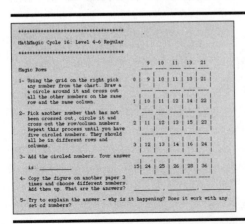

Figure 2.58:
The Magic Rows Puzzle challenge from MathMagic!

Gallery of Interactive Online Geometry

http://www.geom.umn.edu/apps/gallery.html

You can create your own images using seven tools: QuasiTiler, Kali, Orbifold Pinball, Teichmuller Navigator, Cyberview (see Figure 2.59), Unifweb, or Lafite. Each tool site presents an example, which you can use as a starting point. Change variables, and you've got a whole new image. You'll have fun experimenting with and experiencing geometric principles at the same time.

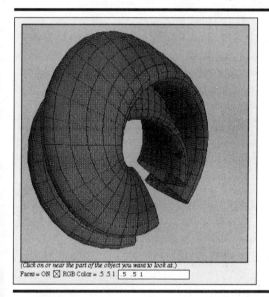

Figure 2.59:
Cyberview-X, after one adjustment

(Click on or near the part of the object you want to look at.)
Faces = ON ☒ RGB Color = .5 .5 1 | .5 .5 1 |

String Figures from Around the World

http://www.ece.ucdavis.edu/~darsie/string.html

First you get a piece of string, then you tie a knot in it so that it makes a large loop, and now you're ready to start. At this site, you'll find string position descriptions, string movement descriptions, illustrations of common openings and endings, as well as beginning and advanced string figures. Beginners can choose from among 13 examples, including Two Coyotes and Two Mountains and a River. After you've worked through the whole set, you'll be ready for the 15 advanced figures, including Asi-Asu (A Double Canoe) from New Guinea,

Four Boys Walking in a Row, an Australian Aborigine figure, and An Apache Door, which is also familiar to Navajo and Pueblo people. Your online teacher has put up less than half his collection, and you can e-mail him for more.

Street Cents Online

http://www.screen.com/streetcents.html

"Street Cents Online is about your money—how to get it and how not to get ripped off when you spend it." That's the message you're given when you first get to this site. Pretty quickly, you'll realize that *Street Cents* is a TV program for kids that can be seen in Canada. The online site builds on what's presented on the show, and you can get scheduling information here. Eighteen topics are covered during the year: music, sports, hair, food, part-time work, school, whining, body, snow, habits, stocks and investing, entertainment, speed, green careers, exaggeration, health, scruples, and water. Each topic leads to another page, where you'll be able to get and share information. For example, you'll most likely find a "Beef of the Week" for each topic, such as an investigation into the high cost of snowboarding (snow) or a look at employers who treat you unfairly (part-time work). You'll also find surveys and their results, viewer letters, and other articles of interest on each topic. One of the "Streetests" included looking at four makes of flannel work shirts, which ranged in price from $5.99 to $24.99. The testers bought two of each shirt, wore one for a week, and washed the other ten times. Based on how they held up in the wash and felt in the wearing, one of the most expensive shirts turned out to be the best bargain, according to these experts.

World Wide Quilting Page

http://ttsw.com/MainQuiltingPage.html

Everything you want to know about quilting is probably here. You'll find How To's, Quilt Blocks, Foundation Blocks, Quilt History, Quilt Stores, Quilt Shows, Fabrics, Computers and Quilting, FAQs, Quilting Guides, and Quilt-Related Mailing Lists, among others. Computers and Quilting gets you to software you can use to design your quilt. You'll find instructions and templates to piece more than a dozen traditional squares, including Ohio Star, Jacob's Ladder, Card Trick, and Storm at Sea (see Figure 2.60). You'll also see a picture of the

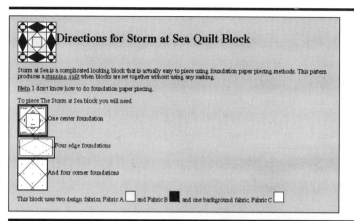

Figure 2.60:
You will find the
pattern for the Storm
at Sea quilt block on
the World Wide
Quilting Page.

winner of the Worst Quilt in the World contest. Contestants are judged on general appearance, color, design, and workmanship. Abominable Mention Awards are also given.

El MOOndo

gsep.pepperdine.edu 7777

login: connect guest

The world of MOOs and MUDs and other such places on the Internet can sometimes be overwhelming. Here's a MOO (multi-object oriented environment) where you can come in, take a look around, and find out what MOOs are all about. MOOs and their like are text-based virtual worlds in which you become a character that moves around, makes decisions, encounters other MOOers, and takes action. This MOO is sponsored by the Graduate School of Education at Pepperdine University in California. It's a fairly new MOO, so the population is about 100. Take a peek; you might like it!

Playing Drool

http://www.mit.edu:8001/afs/athena.mit.edu/user/j/b/jbreiden/game/entry.html

Pretend that you're a dog. Are you a male or a female, or have you been neutered? Are you a mutt, Great Dane, Black Labrador, German Shepherd, dumb yapping poodle, weiner dog, or Snoopy? At any rate, you're playing in the park somewhere in Boston doing your favorite thing: chasing a stick that your master throws. You're running for it, you're going to grab it, but an obnoxious kid grabs it and throws it off in another direction. You can't go back to your master without the stick, so you set off to find it. Thus begin your adventures in this mostly text-based online game. You'll encounter obstacles, twists, and humor as you wend your way through the park that will lead you to success. Some graphics and sound effects are included, but for the most part you'll be selecting directions and following links to get that darn stick.

The Electronic Postcard

http://postcards.www.media.mit.edu/Postcards/

Been wanting to e-mail something a little different to a friend? Here's your chance. You can select a postcard from the rack, which includes some famous artists' works (Van Gogh, Da Vinci, Monet, and Gaugauin, for example), as well as other categories such as graffiti, the holidays, music, images from Vietnam and American cities. You select your card, write a message if you wish, and send it. Your friend will get a message that a postcard is waiting, along with a number. To pick up a card, go to the pick-up window and enter the number. Cards must be picked up within three weeks. Figure 2.61 shows an example of a card from the rack.

Figure 2.61 :
An electronic postcard: Tokyo in the Rain

The LEGO Home Page

http://legowww.homepages.com/

Remember those wonderful red, yellow, and blue pieces that you could put together to make all kinds of things? Well, here's the latest development: Internet information from the company. You'll find out what's new, what's planned, and what some folks have done. There are pictures of home-built constructions, LEGO robots, games with LEGO, projects, ideas, information, and even a LEGO theme song. There's a <u>LEGO Builders Club</u> you can join, a history of LEGOs, and other information sources. You can even tour the Enfield, Connecticut, factory. Did you know that there are 1,610 different LEGO pieces in all?

The Dilbert Zone

http://www.unitedmedia.com/comics/dilbert

Scott Adams's cartoon character, Dilbert, often experiences trials and tribulations in his work world, on and off the Net. At this site, you can see today's cartoon, get into a two-week Dilbert cartoon archive, find a newspaper in your area that carries Dilbert, take a look at the Dilbert Zone FAQ, and see a photo tour of how Scott creates the cartoon. Scott also has a suggestion. If you will make a hand puppet out of a sock and have a photograph taken of you with your hand puppet at your computer, he'll publish it. He insists that talking to the hand puppet will help you reduce any computer-generated stress. Maybe it's worth a try.

FUTUREPLACE, The Park

http://www.itp.tsoa.nyu.edu/~alumni/dlasday/xx/intro.chall.html

You are invited to design a part of FUTUREPLACE, a "new international chain of theme parks." You can choose from three themes and five attractions. Perhaps you'd like to design a ride, a pavilion, an exhibit, a game, or a demonstration. Your park may have an Exploration theme, which will "give visitors a feel for the process of developing and testing a hypothesis and the excitement of discovery." Or maybe it's Lifestyles you're exploring, which will take a look at homes of the future and how they are like or will be different from the homes of today. The Entertainment parks will include your idea of the "entertainment technology" of the future. Check out this site for some designs that have been submitted already, as well as guidelines for submitting your design, which will include a statement of purpose, graphics or rough sketches, construction, and discussion of the design process. (See Figure 2.62 to get a sense of this site.)

Figure 2.62:
Futuristic living is the theme, and you can participate in FUTUREPLACE.

Virtual Frog Dissection Kit

http://george.lbl.gov/ITG.hm.pg.docs/dissect/info.html

At this famous site, you have the chance to dissect a frog in a variety of ways. You decide whether you want to "cut" through a particular area of the frog or see the whole thing. You can select which parts you want to view, such as skeleton or organs, and you can rotate the frog or see it from above or below. You can also click on the various organs to get information about them. A tutorial will take you through a dissection, or you can take off on your own.

The Father of Shareware

http://www.halcyon.com/knopf/jim

Several options are available to you at Jim Knopf's shareware page. You can acquire some freeware written by Jim, including several Windows selections (calendar, CD player, wallpaper changer, wordfind puzzle builder), and you can link to shareware programs for both Macintosh and PC, including The Games Domain, Maui Net Surfin' Software, Windows Shareware Archive, and

The World of Macintosh Shareware. Shareware users and authors will find the page of interest.

Mr. Potato Head

http://winnie.acsu.buffalo.edu/potatoe

Named the Diversion of the Month, May 1995, this Web site is a favorite of a lot of folks, whether they like to create their own versions of the famous character or take a break to laugh a bit. It's a place you should visit at least once. You can play the traditional game in an online version by selecting eyes, ears, nose, mouth, hair, chin, and feet. You'll then see your creation and can start all over again. You can also check out the PotatoeCam Hall of Fame or see some short animations involving the versatile vegetable. (See Figure 2.63 for a shot taken from one of the animations.)

Figure 2.63:
A screen from The Amazing Flying Edible Starchy Tuber Head

WWW Spirograph

http://juniper.tc.cornell.edu:8000/spiro/spiro.html

You can create your own geometric drawing by setting parameters through this site. You decide on the radius of the fixed circle, the radius of the rotating circle, and the offset from the edge of the rotating circle and then watch the image being generated. You'll also see the mathematical equations involved. By making adjustments and drawing new images, you'll get a sense of what happens when you change first one variable and then another. See which combinations you find most satisfying artistically.

Cloud Gallery

http://www.commerce.digital.com/palo-alto/Cloud Gallery/home.html

At this unusual site, you'll find 32 wonderful photographs of clouds. Mary Bartnikowski and Michael Price, professional photographers, have made available some of their favorite pictures. You can download them—they are copyright free—and use them for backgrounds, charts, brochures, newsletters, special effects, or whatever occurs to you. The clouds are also contained on a CD, and purchasing information is available through this site. You'll also find some writing by Mary about angels and how to cloud watch (she suggests you simply lie down "on the ground, back on the grass, and gaze upwards"). You can send comments to Mary and Michael and learn a little about them as seen from each other's eyes. Figure 2.64 gives you an idea of what you'll find here.

Figure 2.64:
A Cloud Gallery offering

KIDS IN ACTION

It's very exciting to participate in special projects such as exploring distant places or tracking the migration of butterflies. It's even more exhilarating to extend the group of participants through the Internet. You really get to see the worldwide implications of your studies.

Rainforest Action Network

http://www.wideopen.igc.apc.org/ran/index.html

Here you'll find the Rainforest Action Network, its mission, and some things you can do about these endangered environments. The Rainforest Action Network, founded in 1985, "works to protect the Earth's rainforests and support the rights of their inhabitants through education, grassroots organizing, and non-violent direct action." At this site, you can get copious rainforest information, including why they are important, an action alert index, a world rainforest report, and rates of rainforest destruction. In the Kids' Corner, you'll learn that your actions can change the world, and you can see eight steps for kids to take (see Figure 2.65), such as don't let anyone in your family buy anything made of ivory, coral, reptile skins, tortoise shells, or cat pelts, and try to choose cereals, cookies, and nuts that are made from rainforest products and advertise their support for rainforest protection. You can also find out about current boycotts and demonstrations.

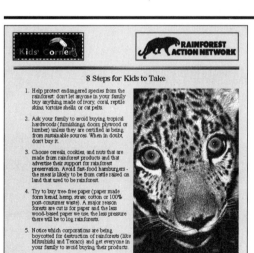

Figure 2.65:
A few steps you can take to help preserve the rainforest

The JASON Project

http://seawifs.gsfc.nasa.gov/JASON.html

Since 1989, Dr. Robert Ballard has conducted scientific expeditions in remote areas of the globe. During the expedition, real-time broadcasts are made to participating groups in the U.S., Canada, Bermuda, and the UK. At these sites, through *telepresence* (being able to operate the on-site scientific equipment through a computer), viewers can go live to the expedition sites, interact with the project robot, JASON, and talk directly with scientists. Past expeditions have been to such sites as the Mediterranean Sea, Lake Ontario (investigating ships from the War of 1812), the Galapagos Islands, and the Sea of Cortez. The Planet Earth expedition visited a rainforest, caverns, Mayan ruins, and the coral reef of Belize. The Island Earth expedition took a look at the environment, volcanoes, and observatories of Hawaii. Coming up is a visit to Southern Florida, focusing on conditions for life in the coastal marine habitats there. At the JASON project Internet site, you'll also have opportunities for online discussions as well as exercises such as Spiders of the World, The Volcanoes of Io, and the Island Migration Simulation Program.

Welcome to the Monarch Watch!

http://129.237.246.134/

Beginning its fourth year, the Monarch Watch project involves students across the monarch migration pattern in tagging and rearing monarch butterflies (*Danaus plexippus*). In 1994, at leat 20,000 students in 30 states tagged and studied monarchs through the program. At this site, you can get membership and ordering information, tag recovery data for the last three years, 1993 and 1994 season summary news (1995 will be online soon), monarch sightings, a Milkweed Handbook (milkweed is a monarch's favorite food), and ideas for making butterfly cages. You can also find out which enemies a monarch has (viruses, bacteria, protozoa, various insects, as well as mice and some birds). (See Figure 2.66 for a glimpse of the home page.)

Welcome to the Monarch Watch! is full of beautiful monarch pictures, which can take a while to load. However, it's well worth the wait to see these lovely butterflies in all stages of their development.

Welcome to the Monarch Watch!

University of Kansas, Department of Entomology

Welcome, this is the fourth year of an outreach program we now call the Monarch Watch. Our goals are to further science education, particularly in primary and secondary school systems, to promote conservation of monarch butterflies and to involve thousands of students and adults in a cooperative study of the monarch's fall migration.

Figure 2.66: Welcome to the Monarch Watch! home page.

The Safari Splash Home Page

http://oberon.educ.sfu.ca/splash.htm

Sponsored by the ExCITE Center and the Royal British Columbia Museum, this 1994 project involved students and research scientists from across Canada. You'll learn about the Safari, read the journal of the five-day expedition, and take a look at the student newsletter. Each student used a powerbook and a Quicktake digital camera to record explorations of such environments as a touch tank of marine animals (they could touch or pick up the creatures), the contents of seine or trawl nets, or what happened while they did some deep-sea diving. You can also get to a 3-D undersea life icon gallery to reach more information, and there are links to associated home pages, such as Charlotte, the Vermont Whale and Shark Images, by Douglas J. Long (see those site descriptions in this book).

You can get the Safari Splash study guide through its Gopher site: cln.etc.bc.ca:70/11/cln/special/safari.

People to Meet

People are what it's all about. It's people who created the Internet, who add information for others to use, and who maintain the sites. One of the most exciting aspects of going online is encountering folks you'd never get to meet any other way. For the cost of a phone call to your Internet provider, you can be online with people all over the world. There are lots of places where people want you to see what they've done, and they invite you to share with them. In this section, you'll find some sites where what you have to say and do is most important.

PEOPLE TO PEOPLE

Kids can make a difference. The sites listed below (and others that you'll surely discover as you travel the Internet) offer opportunities for you to get involved with others. You can discuss ideas, find out from other kids about places you've never been, or work on projects together. Take a look!

Academy One

http://nptn.org/cyber.serv/AOneP/

At this site, you'll find lots to do. You can participate in projects, find keypals, and solve problems. For example, recently Olmsted Falls Middle School challenged participants to build a mouse trap–powered vehicle that would go farther than anyone else's. Last year's winner was Joe L., whose vehicle traveled an impressive 79 feet 2 inches. A current discussion has to do with state rules for getting a driver's license. One project involves building a Kids Online Travel Guide. There are questions you can answer and places to send pictures if you'd like. You can offer to be a keypal, or you can link up with someone else who's already signed up. If you have suggestions or ideas to improve this site, you can send them in as well. (See Figure 2.67 for a look at Academy One.)

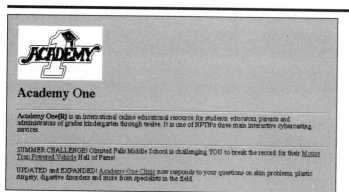

Figure 2.67: Academy One has offered opportunities for kids to connect with kids for a long time. Its Web site extends invitations for more projects.

KIDLINK

kids.ccit.duq.edu

http://kidslink.ccit.duq.edu:70/kidlink-general.html

At KIDLINK you'll find projects, services, and other resources for kids. Probably you'll be most interested in the KIDART Computer Art Gallery and the KIDLINK Projects. You'll find descriptions of past projects, as well as ongoing and new ones. For example, KIDS-96 is a "grassroots project aimed at getting as many children in the age group 10–15 as possible involved in a global dialog." KIDS-96 was started in 1990, and since then, more than 37,000 kids from 71 countries and all continents have participated. To participate, you'll thoughtfully answer four questions: Who am I? What do I want to be when I grow up? How do I want to make the world to be better when I grow up? What can I do now to make this happen? You'll be able to see what other kids have said and even join the KIDCAFE, where you can connect with keypals and participate in a number of discussions. You can find KIDCAFE in four languages: Japanese, Portuguese, Scandinavian (Nordic), and Spanish. You can also participate in other KIDLINK projects, such as KIDFORUM and KIDPROJ. There's lots to learn about and do at this site, and here you can meet many, many other kids.

Britannica Online

http://www.eb.com/

You may think this section of the book a strange place to find this site, but it's the people connection I want to focus on. You can get to Encyclopedia Britannica's resources if you subscribe (Grolier's Encyclopedia can be found online as well at another site), and you can find out how to do that at this site. But the thing I liked a lot was the Britannica's Lives section. You'll find short biographies of people who have birthdays on the date you go to the site. You can also find other people who have birthdays in the same year, and those references are linked to others that have the same date. For example, Peggy Fleming's birthday is July 27, 1948. I read a little about her, then clicked on the year, and found Anatoly Scharansky, whose birthday is January 20, 1948. After finding out a bit about who he is, I could click on January 20 and find others with that birthday during different years. You can select another day or year as well. I liked this site as a starting place for learning about interesting people.

I*EARN

http://www.igc.apc.org/iearn

The International Education and Resource Network (I*EARN) is a special, worldwide group of educators and students (which you can also join). Its members develop and collaborate on projects that build awareness about issues the world's peoples are facing. It's designed for kids ages 6–19, and projects have been implemented in many countries of the world. You can reach home pages for I*EARN Australia, I*EARN España, I*EARN North America Mid-Continent Center, and I*EARN North American Pacific Northwest Center. You can take a look at student projects, such as A Day in the Life, First/Indigenous Peoples, Kids Can Newsletter, and Arctic to Amazon Recovery, a conference that will facilitate cooperative interaction among young people in recovery from alcohol and/or drug abuse. You can go directly to the I*EARN Gopher, where you can find current I*EARN project descriptions, as well as completed I*EARN projects with evaluations. If you're interested in meeting other kids who, like yourself, want to do something good for themselves, other people, and the planet, check out I*EARN's home page.

SCHOOLS AND CLASSROOMS

More and more schools and classrooms can be found on the Internet. The World Wide Web has made it all possible. Here you'll find a small sample of the growing list of participants.

Web66 WWW Schools Registry

http://hillside.coled.umn.edu/others.html

More schools than you ever thought existed have home pages on the Web. Take a look at this site to find lists of them and links to Country School Listings, Global School Listings, Elementary Schools, Secondary Schools, School Districts, Educational Organizations, and K-12 School Lists. You'll also find Public Libraries on the Internet, Post-Secondary Institutions Worldwide, and United States Post-Secondary Institutions. From an alphabetic list, you can click on a letter to get more information. For example, I clicked on the letter *I* and got 35 listings, from Ijselland Polytechnic in the Netherlands, through such places as the Indiana Institute of Technology in Madras, Indiana University in Bloomington, the Institut National des Telecommunications, the International Islamic University, Malayasia, to Ithaca College. Incidentally, if your local library isn't online, you might want to tell your librarian about this site and find out if the library has plans to become a part of it.

Steve Stratford's K-12 All-Stars

http://www.umich.edu/~sstrat/BestK12.html

Steve has selected 12 schools that have developed outstanding home pages on the Net. His Grand Prize winner is Patch American High School, in Stuttgart, Germany (see the entry later in this section). Each winner is listed, along with a link to the site showing off something special there. Other winners include Smoky Hill High School in Aurora, Colorado, for Best Student-Run; Gonzaga College High School in Washington, DC, for Most Incredible Student Projects; and Monte Vista High School in Danville, Colorado, for Most Promising. Ralph Bunche School in Harlem (see the entry later in this section) took the Incredible Elementary Kids prize. (See Figure 2.68 for a look at this page.)

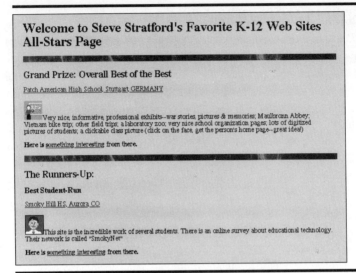

Figure 2.68:
Steve Stratford's
K-12 All-Stars home
page connects you
directly to the
award-winning
schools through
the Something
Interesting link.

Melrose School

http://ousd.k12.ca.us/melrose/melrose.html

Melrose School's home page includes stories and pictures by fifth- and sixth-grade students in Portable E at Melrose School in Oakland, California. Among other work, you'll find Rosy's short biography of Diego Rivera in English and Spanish, Mayra's and Guillermo's versions of school memories, and Yen's "Watermelon Book," which includes sketches she made while writing the story. "El Libro Anaranjado," by Octavio, Leticia, and Juan, includes 14 pages of drawings that illustrate a number sentence. For example, you'll find that "Naranjo número cinco fue a México" and that "Naranjo número nueve fue a escuela."

Ralph Bunche School (RBS)

http://mac94.ralphbunche.rbs.edu/

This interesting school in Harlem, New York, was the first to put up its own Gopher site several years ago. Now you can visit its home page, where'll you find many selections. You can find out What's New at RBS, check out Good Places to Find Other Student Work, see the Spanish alphabet that was illustrated by students (see Figure 2.69 for an example), learn about projects students have worked on, and get access to Gopher files containing the school's newsletter. Perhaps you'll enjoy the Pineapple Project—a project developed at Teachers College, Columbia University, in which seven schools (including RBS) participated. Students at each school tracked what was involved in shipping produce from one part of the country to another. Students also looked at ways in which early native people in their areas obtained food without our trains, planes, and trucks. You'll find a map showing the participating schools and links to each. Students at RBS have found many interesting resources on the Internet, which are listed, with links for you to follow.

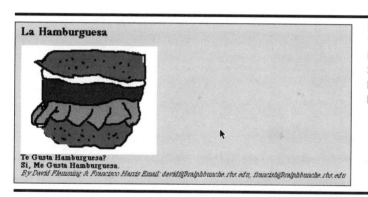

La Hamburguesa

Te Gusta Hamburguesa?
Si, Me Gusta Hamburguesa.
By David Flemming & Francisco Harris Email: davidf@ralphbunche.rbs.edu, franciscf@ralphbunche.rbs.edu

Figure 2.69:
"La Hamburguesa,"
by Ralph Bunche
School's David
Flemming and
Francisco Harris

Hoffer Elementary School

http://cmp1.ucr.edu/exhibitions/cmp_ed_prog.html

Meet the third-grade students from Room 8, Hoffer Elementary School in Banning, California. Their school has been part of a photography project in which they've been working with video and still cameras for a number of years. You can see them, hear them, and look at what they've done with photo montage, animation, and video. They also share the results of an e-mail book project with Murphy Ranch School and an Internet wind experiment.

The Salmon Page–Riverdale School

http://www.riverdale.k12.or.us/salmon.html

At this site, students share their research and reports on salmon studies (see Figure 2.70). You'll find fifth-graders Chris and John's Life Cycle of a Salmon, the daily fish passage report, a link to the <u>World Wide Web Virtual Library: Fish</u>, a fish FAQ, information on how and where to get smoked salmon via the Internet, how to subscribe to the Salmon Listserv, and the Endangered Species Act write-up. You can also connect to the school's more general home page to see what the rest of the students at the school are up to.

The Salmon Page

Dedicated to all things salmon:
How to catch them, cook them, buy them and save them...

Figure 2.70:
Riverdale School's students share their salmon project on the Internet through The Salmon Page.

Captain Strong Elementary

http://152.157.16.3/doc/salmon/salmon1.html

This address will take you to the Salmon Project, which has involved third-grade students at the school for several years. You can learn about five kinds of salmon and two kinds of trout, hazards that fish encounter, and development stages of fish. Available here is a 35 megabyte HyperCard stack built for students in the Battle Ground School District (BGSD). You can also get to the BGSD home page, the elementary page, and teacher resources and find out what's new in the district.

Buckman School

http://www.buckman.pps.k12.or.us/buckman.html

Not only are Buckman students regularly traveling the Web, they're experimenting with video over the Net. Through their <u>Almost Live from Room 100</u>, you'll be able to see a picture taken every three minutes by a QuickCam. Students have also participated in video conferencing sessions with people such as a woman from Beijing and Craig Hickman, the author of KidPix (a popular computer art program). You could also participate in the Penny Web: Guess the number of pennies in their penny jar. More than 100 guesses came from all over the U.S., Mexico, Canada, Bermuda, Germany, Israel, and Australia. Fabian, from Munich, Germany, submitted the winning guess of 12,584 and gets the Buckman School Travel Mug. There are other projects, art, and student writing, as well as current weather information and the results of the Humpty Dumpty Eggdrop Challenge (28 eggs made it; 10 didn't).

Patch American High School

http://192.253.114.31/Home.html

This school is in Stuttgart, Germany, and holds the Grand Prize from Steve Stratford's Favorite K-12 All-Stars page (read more about this site at the beginning of this *Schools and Classrooms* section). A U.S. Department of Defense school, Patch is the first high school to put up a Web server in Europe (see Figure 2.71). When you visit the site, you can take a quick tour and then check out the Academics section, which includes <u>Arab-Israeli Conflict</u>, <u>Biology</u>, <u>Computer Science</u>, <u>German</u>, <u>Internet Class</u>, <u>Music</u>, <u>Social Studies</u>, <u>Student Art Gallery</u>, and <u>Video Production</u>. Patch's multicurricular projects include World War II, Stereograms, and Partner Schools. You can take virtual field trips to Stuttgart, Augsburg, Maulbronn Abbey, Patch Barracks (both before and after World War II), Rasel during carnival season, Vietnam through the eyes of an American, and the Mercedes-Benz and Porsche museums. You can see some of the school through pictures and a movie and read reports by three students on virtual reality and its future uses on the Net and in the world. Patch's featured project, Berlin Wall Falls: Perspectives From 5 Years Down the Road, will include thoughts and ideas from people. They're looking for as many as 30 sites to participate. You and your school can join the project by contacting them through this site.

Patch American High School

Home of the first High School Web server in Europe. *Online since March 22, 1994*

Celebrating our first year on the Web!

Welcome to Patch American High School, located at Patch Barracks, Headquarters for US EUCOM, the United States European Command, in Vaihingen, a small section of Stuttgart, Germany.

Built in 1979, Patch is a testbed site for technology insertion programs in the Department of Defense Dependents Schools system. The post and school are named after Lt. General Alexander M. Patch.

As exemplified by our mascot the Panther, students and teachers at Patch are always *on the prowl* for exciting ways to improve our school and community. This home page, under development by students working in a number of projects, can link you to a variety of resources in the school, in the DoDDS system, and around the world.

 Take a look at the newest additions to our WWW server or take a quick tour.

Figure 2.71:
Visit Patch American High School's home page and learn about the school and online projects.

American Commemorative Postage Stamp Designs

http: www.inform.umd.edu:8080/UMS+State/UMD-Projects/MCTP/Technology/
School_WWW_Pages/

Although this site wins the award for "longest Web address," when you get there, you'll be glad you did. Mrs. O'Haver's fifth-grade class at Fairland Elementary School in Montgomery County, Maryland, designed postage stamps using Native American motifs. You'll see representations of Southwest, Eastern Woodland, Plains, and Pacific Coast Indian life and art. For example, there are Southwest Indian rugs and blankets, Kachinas, pottery, and housing and land drawings, as well as symbols, such as the lizard, Mother Earth and the Snake Dance, Bald Eagles, Gourd Rattles, and an Interesting Storyteller Doll (see Figure 2.72 for an example).

Figure 2.72:
A Kachina doll
stamp design

Kachina doll

This stamp commorates a Kachina doll. That is a type of person that lived in the underworld. He taught the people how to live such as planting corn or being thankful for what they have. The Southwest Indians beleved in these supernatural beings. They were a mix of man and god. A Kachina doll is made of cottonwood. The children keep them for good luck.

Vishal Bhatnagar.

Click here to return to the Index.

SPECIAL FRIENDS

Another interesting area on the Internet is the growing collection of resources for people with disabilities. Along with the National Library Service for the Blind and Physically Handicapped cited in the *Government Issue* section of this book, you'll find online places to go for information and to share with others, as well as links to more sites.

Leeder O. Men

http://www.rain.org/~lytle/leeder.html

At this great site, you'll find The Heart Warming Adventures of Leeder O. Men, your favorite wheelchair stuntman, by John Lytle (see Figure 2.73). A number of John's pictures show Leeder as he engages in his favorite sports— surfing, mountain climbing, and skateboarding. You can write the artist, who is currently publishing a book about Leeder's feats.

WebABLE!

http://www.webable.com/

This site calls itself "the Web's first-stop-shop for people with disabilities." It offers a quarterly newsletter, a directory of services for listservs, FTP and Gopher sites, product catalogs, and links to other accessibility and disability

Figure 2.73:
Leeder O. Men rides the waves.

Web sites. You'll find links to <u>Research Centers and Projects</u>, <u>Education</u>, <u>General Disability Sites</u>, <u>Associations and Non-profit Organizations</u>, <u>Product Solution Providers</u>, and <u>Grants</u>. Take a peek. Chances are you'll find connections to what you're looking for.

Deaf World Web

http://deafworldweb.org/deafworld/

The goal of this site is to "maintain information available on the deaf around the world and to provide free services to the individuals, researchers, and non-profit organizations worldwide—to eliminate the ignorance, oppression, fear, and approach of subtle eugenics." You'll find two main areas: <u>Deaf Culture</u> and <u>References</u>. By clicking on Deaf Culture, you'll get to anecdotes, articles, history, language, literature, and voices. Jokes and newsletters will be included soon, and submissions to the site in all areas are encouraged. Through References, you can get to arts and entertainment, education, Internet, media, organizations, researchers' forum, services, sports and recreation, technology, and miscellaneous. Each section offers abundant information. For example, under education, you can choose from universities, technical institutions (in

Canada and the U.S.), sign language courses, schools for the deaf (in Canada, Japan, the U.S., and Manilla School in Sweden). You'll find a Question of the Week, which you can answer online. For example, if you are deaf, what do you prefer to be called (deaf, hard of hearing, hearing impaired, or other)? The question can also be answered by hearing people: What do you prefer to call deaf people? You can fill in your answer on the form that's provided. This site has comprehensive links and offers an excellent service to the deaf community. (See Figure 2.74 for some of the options.)

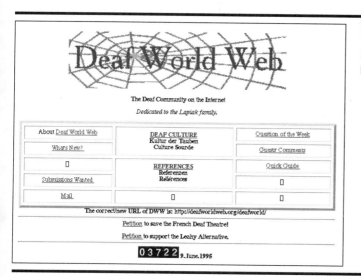

Figure 2.74:
Welcome to the
Deaf World Web
home page.

Disability Resources from Evan Kemp Associates

http://disability.com/

Although this site was designed by a commercial venture, you'll find lots and lots of resources here, and no one tries to do a hard-sell on products. The many categories include News and Information Tips, Disability Mall, Free Guide to Consumer Protection, One Step Ahead Newsletter, Disability Marketing Group, FAQs, Division Medical, and Cool Disability Places, which has links to national and international sites. You can find out about disability resources in Japan, the United Kingdom, and Ireland, for example. There's even a connection to the International Wheelchair Aviators. A Disability Info Tip for the Month might let you know about a free sample issue of a magazine written for 8- to 14-year-olds who have hearing disabilities.

TAAD Center

http://www.interaccess.com/users/taad

TAAD stands for Technical Aids and Assistance for Persons with Disabilities. The group has created an online resource "for making informed decisions about personal computers." There's information about the TAAD Center, a Computer Guide, an online newsletter (TAAD BITS), and related links. The Computer Guide section looks at such issues as why personal computers are important to persons with disabilities and what people can do with computers. In addition, there is an overview of software, information on how to access a personal computer, a discussion about voice recognition systems, and a list of communication aids.

ONE WORLD

The world became a smaller place when astronauts viewed it from space. It's shrunk even more now that we can exchange ideas with people online from nearly every country in the world. The following sites are just a few of the many that actively work toward world peace in the world and global community.

Friends and Partners

http://solar.rtd.utk.edu/friends/home.html

One of the fascinating aspects of connecting to the Internet is the friends in far-away places you meet online. At this site, you'll have a chance to learn about Russia and the Russian people through information shared in the hope of building global friendships and understanding. The opening clickable map offers topics such as history, geography, art/music, literature, language, telecommunications, education, science, and life. Each section contains a large amount of information and resources. For example, if you select Life, you'll have options to join a Family Chat Corner, read a brief biography of Oksana Bayul, see images of Uzbekistan, get to the Russian Football Homepage, check out the Pen Pal Forum, and visit the Moscow Children Computer Club. This site truly builds more than electronic links between Russia and the U.S.. (See Figure 2.75 for a look at the Cyrillic alphabet found at this site.)

З	з	zeh		z in zoo	z	
И	и	ee	•	ee in see	ee	
Й	й	ee krahtkoᵞeh	•	y in boy	y	
К	к	kah		k in kitten	k	
Л	л	ehl		l in lamp	l	
М	м	ehm		m in my	m	
Н	н	ehn		n in not	n	
О	о	o	•	o in hot	o	
П	п	peh		p in pot	p	
Р	p	ehr		trilled (like scottish r)	r	
С	с	ehs		like s in see	s/ss	
Т	т	teh		t in tip	t	
У	v	oo	•	oo in boot	oo	
Ф	ф	ehf		f in face	f	
Х	x	khah		ch in Scottish loch	kh	
Ц	ц	tseh		ts in sits	ts	
Ч	ч	chᵞah		ch in chip	chᵞ	
Ш	ш	shah		sh in shut	sh	

Figure 2.75:
Learning each other's languages helps build friendships. The Russian (Cyrillic) alphabet shown at this site illustrates some basic differences between English and Russian.

Oneworld Online

http://www.bbcnc.org.uk/online/oneworld/top.htm

This site describes itself as "a meeting place for the one world community... Our aim is to make available—free and worldwide—some of the best thinking, writing, picture-taking and broadcasting about global themes currently being produced." You'll find links to education sites, information about television, radio, video, CD-ROMs and how to order them, books, special activities, conferences, and reports. For example, the full transcript of a Save the Children Fund Report, "Towards a Children's Agenda—New Challenges for Social Development," is available online. You can also read short papers by the late Jim Grant, Executive Director of UNICEF, and by Frederico Mayor, UNESCO Director-General. This is a good site for getting involved with human rights issues and learning about what's being done.

Human Rights Web Home Page

http://www.traveller.com/~hrweb/hrweb.html

This site presents you with several engaging sections: human rights emergencies, information about human rights and the human rights movement, suggestions for action, human rights resources page, and the human rights Web administrative page. You'll find biographies of prisoners of conscience, human rights legal and political documents, and a section on human rights issues, debates, and discussions. You can take a look at A Primer for New Human Rights Activists, and you'll find links to human rights organizations you can join. This site offers a fine collection of information on this important topic (see Figure 2.76).

Figure 2.76:
The Human Rights Web Home Page offers many opportunities for informing ourselves and participating in meaningful human rights activities.

Acts of injustice done
     between the setting and the rising sun
In history lie like bones,
    each one.

    -- W. H. Auden, *"The Ascent of F6"*

The Human Rights Web Home Page

Select the bullet to see a short description of the page, or the topic itself to go directly to that page. Header pages don't have descriptions, either because their content should be obvious from the title or because no short description will do the job.

HUMAN RIGHTS EMERGENCIES

WHAT ARE HUMAN RIGHTS?

- *An Introduction to Human Rights*
- *A Short History of the Human Rights Movement*
- *Biographies of Prisoners of Conscience*
- *Human Rights Legal and Political Documents*

World-Wide Web Virtual Library: United Nations and Other International Organizations

 http://undcp.org/unlinks.html

At this site, you can get information about the United Nations, and you'll find links to many organizations. What's New? contains links to sites that have been added, listing most recent additions first. You'll find links to such places as the World Intellectual Property Organization and the International Year of Tolerance and a link to the World Food Program Gopher. You can also search by keyword through the United Nations General Assembly and Security Council resolutions. There is a section on the United Nations 50th anniversary celebrations, including links to the UN50 Closing Ceremony and M-BONE broadcast, Dialogues of Peace: Art for UN50, and UN50 in San Francisco. You'll also find links related to the site under categories such as activism, conferences, human rights, and international affairs.

Net Tools

There's a story about a king who wanted to reward a young kitchen helper for some important task she accomplished that no one else could do. This girl was also very clever (and had been good at math since she was young), so she asked the king if he would double her wages every day for a month. Since she only made a penny a day, the king (who wasn't very good at math) agreed instantly. The first day, the girl got her penny. The second day, she got two pennies. The third day she got four pennies, and the fourth day she got eight pennies. By the end of one week, she'd gotten 64 cents. By the end of the second week, the king had to give her $80.32. She got $10,280.96 by the end of the third week, and by the time the month was up, that smart young woman had earned more than $1,000,000.

This story reminds me of what happens when you start looking around on the Internet. Sometimes I think I'm looking for one topic, but when I get to a site that includes it, something is listed that I hadn't even thought of, so I start to explore it. Which takes me to another new place, with lists of other possibilities. Pretty soon it feels as if I've seen a million places, which can feel good or bad. The good part is the fun I've had exploring, and the bad part is feeling overwhelmed with all the places to go. One kind of tool that can help you organize yourself or your travels on the Web is called a *search engine*. Several famous ones are discussed in this section; they can help you get where you want to go—with occasional side trips of your own choosing.

WORLD WIDE WEB LISTS

As you've surely discovered, finding where you want to go on the Internet can be tricky. The sites in this section will give you one kind of help.

TradeWare Galaxy

http://galaxy.einet.net

EINet Galaxy Directory Services provides lists of sites of interest to kids, parents, and teachers, including Interesting Places for Kids, Kid's Web, African American Directory, and Armadillo's K-12 Resources. This site gives you access to a large database of resources that you can search by keywords. You can also limit the number of resources you'll get back, as well as naming the kind you want (World Wide Web, Gopher, and so on) or selecting a combination.

The Best of WWW Contest

http://wings.buffalo.edu/contest

The purpose of this site is to "promote the Web to new/potential users by showing its highlights." Visitors to this site nominated and voted for their choices, and you'll find 1994's winners, along with preliminary information about BoWeb '95. Most winners averaged about 100 votes, and 5100 votes were cast in this contest. General awards include Best Overall Site and WWW Hall of Fame. Application awards go to best educational service and best navigational aid. Technical awards include best document design, best use of multiple media, and most technical merit. For each category, there are honorable mentions and other nominees. You might be interested to know that voters judged the National Center for Supercomputing Applications (http://www.ncsa.uiuc.edu) as the Best Overall Site. Hall of Famers include Tim Berners-Lee, who is "responsible for the very existence of the World Wide Web," since he developed the programming language and protocols that people use on the Internet, as well as Marc Andreessen, Eric Bina, Rob Hartill, Kevin Hughes, and Lou Montulli (chief developer of Lynx). Read about the winners' accomplishments at this site, and find links to their home pages. Incidentally, the Best Educational Site award went to Introduction to Object-Oriented Programming Using C++ (which combines a MOO and HTML hypertextbook). (See Figure 2.77 for a view of this site.)

Want to know about all the servers in the world? Take a look at W3 Servers at http://www.w3.org/hypertext/Datasources/WWW/Geographical.html. *You'll find a list of World Wide Web servers, alphabetically by continent, country, and state. The database includes 56 countries and 47 states. Now you can find out if there's a there there.*

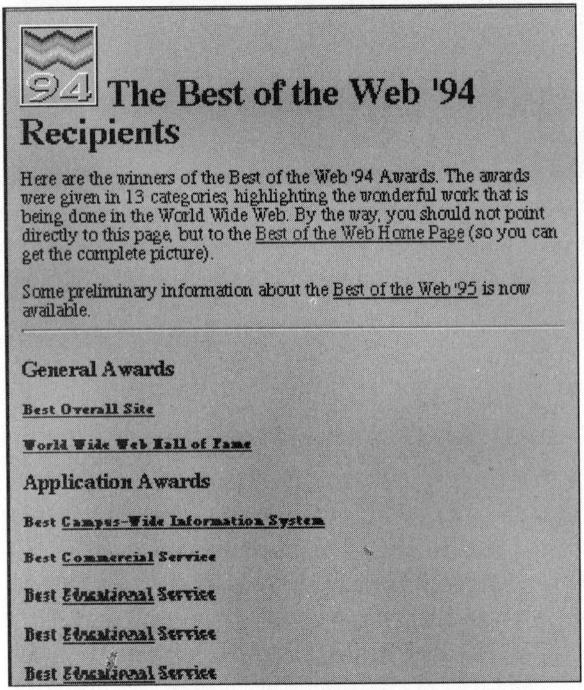

The Best of the Web '94 Recipients

Here are the winners of the Best of the Web '94 Awards. The awards were given in 13 categories, highlighting the wonderful work that is being done in the World Wide Web. By the way, you should not point directly to this page, but to the Best of the Web Home Page (so you can get the complete picture).

Some preliminary information about the Best of the Web '95 is now available.

General Awards

Best Overall Site

World Wide Web Hall of Fame

Application Awards

Best Campus-Wide Information System

Best Commercial Service

Best Educational Service

Best Educational Service

Best Educational Service

Figure 2.77:
Best of the Web home page briefly explains the contest and lists finalists.

The Yahoo Collection

http://www.yahoo.com/

Developed by some graduate students at Stanford University, Yahoo has quickly become *the* searchable collection of Internet sites. You can search by narrowing from large categories to specific entries. The large categories include art, business, computers, economy, education, entertainment, environment and natural events, government, health, humanities, law, news, politics, reference, regional information, science, social science, and society and culture. You'll see the number of entries behind each category that you can get to, which range from 120 for events to 20,532 for business. By the way, Yahoo is actually an acronym for Yet Another Hierarchically Odoriferous Oracle, but it's nice that it's there when you need it!

The World-Wide Web
Virtual Library: Subject Catalogue

http://www.w3.org/hypertext/DataSources/bySubject/Overview.html

You've probably already visited this catalogue, perhaps without even knowing it. For example, in the *Music* section of this book, you'll find a reference to the WWW Virtual Library: Music. This huge collection of Internet sites is divided into categories, listed alphabetically from aboriginal studies to zoos (see Figure 2.78). By going deeper through links, you'll be able to get to the exact place you want to be. You can also connect to other virtual libraries at this site.

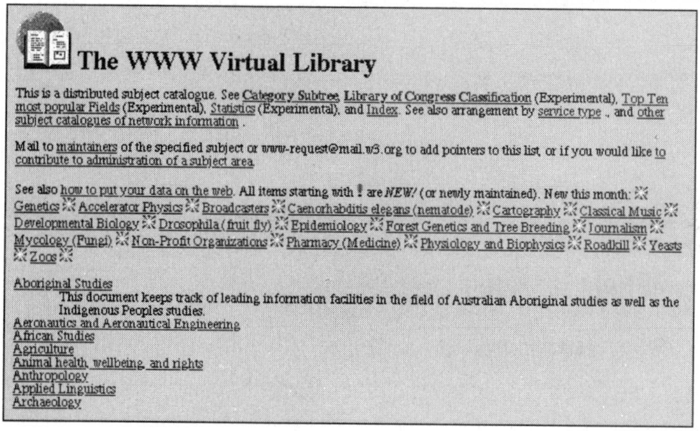

The WWW Virtual Library

This is a distributed subject catalogue. See Category Subtree, Library of Congress Classification (Experimental), Top Ten most popular Fields (Experimental), Statistics (Experimental), and Index. See also arrangement by service type , and other subject catalogues of network information .

Mail to maintainers of the specified subject or www-request@mail.w3.org to add pointers to this list, or if you would like to contribute to administration of a subject area.

See also how to put your data on the web. All items starting with ! are *NEW!* (or newly maintained). New this month: Genetics · Accelerator Physics · Broadcasters · Caenorhabditis elegans (nematode) · Cartography · Classical Music · Developmental Biology · Drosophila (fruit fly) · Epidemiology · Forest Genetics and Tree Breeding · Journalism · Mycology (Fungi) · Non-Profit Organizations · Pharmacy (Medicine) · Physiology and Biophysics · Roadkill · Yeasts · Zoos ·

Aboriginal Studies
This document keeps track of leading information facilities in the field of Australian Aboriginal studies as well as the Indigenous Peoples studies.
Aeronautics and Aeronautical Engineering
African Studies
Agriculture
Animal health, wellbeing, and rights
Anthropology
Applied Linguistics
Archaeology

Figure 2.78:
The WWW Virtual Library home page immediately gives you several ways to access information.

Yanoff's Special Internet Connections

http://www.uwm.edu/Mirror/inet.services.html

Scott Yanoff has been cruising the Net for years, locating good sites and sharing them online. At this site, you'll find 41 topics to search. Scott offers the traditional subject listings such as art and chemistry and then includes categories for such topics as FTP, games/fun/chat, Gopher, Internet, Software, User Lookup Services, and Setting up WWW Servers. You might want to browse his list for topics that may not have occurred to you! (See Figure 2.79.)

Special Internet Connections
Last update 8/2/95

All Pages © 1995 Scott Yanoff
You may email me with submissions/corrections:
yanoff@alpha2.csd.uwm.edu

- AGRICULTURE
- ART
- ASTRONOMY
- AVIATION
- BIOLOGY
- BOTANY
- BUSINESS/ECONOMICS/FINANCIAL
- CHEMISTRY
- COLLEGE PREP
- COMPUTERS
- CONSUMER/COMMERCIAL INFORMATION/RESOURCES
- EDUCATION/TEACHING/LEARNING
- EMPLOYMENT
- FOOD/RECIPES/COOKING
- FTP
- GAMES/FUN/CHAT
- GEOPHYSICAL/GEOGRAPHICAL/GEOLOGICAL
- GOPHER
- GOVERNMENT/POLITICS
- HISTORY
- INTERNET
- LAW
- LITERATURE/BOOKS/LANGUAGES

Figure 2.79:
Scott Yanoff's home page offers another way of organizing online information.

The Whole Internet Catalog

http://nearnet.gnn.com/wic/newrescat.toc.html

At this site, you'll be able to search the Internet by topics such as arts and entertainment, Internet, and travel. You can also find out what's new, get to a celebrity hotlist, check out the top 50 sites, or go to all catalog entries. Follow the links until you get to where you want to go.

INTERNET INFORMATION

Even veteran Internet travelers can profit from tips and tricks for navigating the online world. The sites in this section offer information about the Internet and finding your way around it.

The Internet Companion

http://www.obs-us.com/obs/english/books/editinc/obsxxx.htm

At this Web site, you'll find an online version of Tracy Laquey's book, *The Internet Companion*. You can choose by chapter and topic what you'd like to explore. For example, there's information about the Internet itself, why you might want to get online, how to get connected, and how to find online resources and use e-mail. One fascinating chapter, "Internet in-the-Know Guide," includes such topics as games, security issues, and legends on the Net. You may prefer to buy the book and read it outside by the pool. Or you may be intrigued by an online book about the online world.

The Internet Index, an online compilation of interesting Net-related facts, can be found at http://www.openmarket.com/info/internet-index/95-06.html. In this edition, you could find out that there are 4 Internet access providers in Egypt, 25 PBS stations that have Web home pages, and the phone number for information about the National Information Infrastructure (1-800-NII-8818).

World Wide Web Workbook

http://sln.fi.edu/tfi/primer/primer.html

At this site, which is part of the Franklin Science Institute, you can explore the basic ins and outs of the World Wide Web. In five lessons (Hypertext, Graphics, Hypergraphics, Imagemaps, and Interactivity), you'll get a brief explanation of each of these Web features, as well as HTML. (See below for specifics about HTML programming.)

Information Bank: WWW by Subject

http://www.clark.net/pub/global/front.html

Here you'll find 700 links arranged alphabetically and by subject. The Internet Table of Contents includes compilations of interesting places to visit on the Internet, what's new on the Internet, about the Internet, search the Internet, find persons and addresses, interactive applications, Internet learning and training tools, and current events.

Model High School Mosaic Server

http://www.BLOOMFIELD.K12.MI.US

At this site, you'll find several interesting sections, including <u>About MHS</u>, <u>Internet Resources</u>, <u>Electronic Arts</u>, <u>Computer Center</u>, <u>Phone Books</u>, and <u>Newspaper</u>. The reason this site is listed in this part of the book is the Internet Resources part. You'll find an Internet Safari—an interactive multimedia presentation for finding out all about the Internet and what to do once you're there. You can preview or download the 35 megabyte project, developed by 3 students during 500 hours of work.

SEARCHING, SEARCHING, SEARCHING

Sometimes you may not have the time to move from site to site as you see new links that sound interesting. Perhaps you are searching for specific information. Here is a selection of search tools that will help you find what you're looking for on the Internet.

W3 Search Engines

http://cuiwww.unige.ch/meta-index.html

This site collects search engines for you to connect to. They're arranged in lists, with spaces for you to enter your word or words. You'll then be linked directly to the tool you've chosen, with the results of the search. You'll find List-based WWW Catalogs, such as CUI World Wide Web Catalog, and Spider-based WWW Catalogs, such as WebCrawler and WWW Worm. Other catalogs include Lycos, The Whole Internet Catalog, and WAIS. You can also get to sections titled Software, People, Publications, News/FAQs, Documentation, and Other Interesting Things. For one-stop search shopping, check it out.

When you start searching, you'll probably encounter the following message on your computer:

The information you have submitted is insecure and could be observed by a third party while in transit. If you are submitting passwords, credit card numbers, or other information you would like to keep private, it would be safer for you to cancel the submission.

· *Then you'll get a chance to click on three places: Don't show again, Cancel, or OK. It's nice to get the warning, but for such searches, you might as well click on Don't show again; otherwise, you'll see the same message every time you search.*

The Lycos Home Page: Hunting WWW Information

http://lycos.cs.cmu.edu/

Billed as The Catalog of the Internet and developed by the Carnegie Mellon Foundation, this is one of the very popular search engines. You can choose to search the big Lycos catalog (which looks at 5.07 million Web pages) or the small Lycos catalog (which checks a mere 434 Web pages). You can also use a search form, on which you can enter the number of documents you'd like, as well as other options. When your search is successful, the first ten will show up on the screen, and you'll see such information as the URL, file date, title of the site, and an excerpt. You'll be linked to the site so that you can check it out directly. You'll find out how many hits you got, and you can get to the next ten documents by pressing a key. You can also find out about employment opportunities at Lycos, look at FAQs, and learn how to register and delete your own pages. (See Figure 2.80 for a view of the Lycos home page.)

Figure 2.80: Lycos is one of the most popular search tools on the Internet.

WWWW—World Wide Web Worm

http://www.cs.colorado.edu/home/mcbryan/WWWW.html

A very popular search tool, the WWW Worm takes keywords you give it and looks in the titles of essentially all Web documents to try to find a match. Currently, it checks about 3,000,000 URLs, and about 2,000,000 people use it every month. At the site, you'll find instructions for use, definitions of terms, and examples. You can set the number of matches you'd like to 5, 50, 500, or 5000. When you've gotten a match, you'll see the title or place where the reference was found, and you can jump there through the link provided. (See Figure 2.81 for an example of how to search the Net using the WWW Worm.)

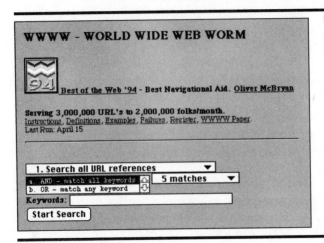

Figure 2.81:
A screen from the World Wide Web Worm

WebCrawler

http://www.biotech.washington.edu/WebCrawler/WebQuery.html

At this site, you enter the word or words you are looking for, and you'll get 25 matches. You can set a different number of hits—10, 100, or 500. This tool searches the body of documents as well as their titles for your terms, so you may get a better result than with tools that look only at URLs. You'll also be able to get FAQs, check the news, try random links, and see the top 25 sites. You can also submit pages to this site, which will be added to the database.

CUI W3 Catalog

http://cuiwww.unige.ch/w3catalog

This site offers a different kind of search. Enter a search word or pattern, and you'll get a title, which is linked to the site. You'll also be told where the site is, but there's no description.

You'll probably find that you end up liking one or two tools best. You might want to try out several, using the same word or term, to get a feel for what happens with each. You might find that one tool is often busy and that another works better or faster.

InfoSeek

http://www.infoseek.com

The format of this site makes it simple to use. Just enter your word or words, and you'll see what matches. The first 10 will be displayed, along with a brief description or taste of the site and its URL. If there were no matches, it's suggested that you read a bit about how to narrow your search. The site is currently available at no charge for the first 10 matches to your search, but you can subscribe to get a larger number of matched sites, and the fee schedule is given.

WAIS

wais.com
login: wais

http://www.wais.com

WAIS, the Wide Area Information Server, has been around for a long time, helping people find things on the Net long before the World Wide Web made locating information so easy. If you use a WAIS Telnet site, you'll enter a text-based environment. If you use the Web, you'll see more familiar buttons on which to click. But you search both in the same way, and both will get you to the same resources. You enter a keyword or words, and you'll get information about databases that might meet your requirements, rather than the documents themselves. You'll get information about how large the database is and the likelihood that it meets your parameters in the form of a score (1000 indicating a perfect match). From there, you can decide which databases you'd like to check, or you can refine your search. (See Figure 2.82 for an example of a WAIS screen.)

Figure 2.82:
WAIS in action

YOU'RE ON THE NET!

If you're thinking about creating your own home page or just curious to see how it's done, the following sites will show you. You'll also find out about such refinements as creating forms in your page and adding attractive backgrounds.

Beginner's Guide to HTML

http://www.gnn.com/gnn/wic/html.03.html

Here's an online book with instructions for learning HTML, the Hypertext Markup Language used to create Web documents. You'll find chapters such as Creating HTML Documents, Linking to Other Documents, Additional Markup Tags, and In-line Images. When you're ready to publish your own pages, here's a place to start. The extensive table of contents you'll see at the home page lets you start at the very beginning or jump to a topic you need to write your page. See Figure 2.83 and start to work!

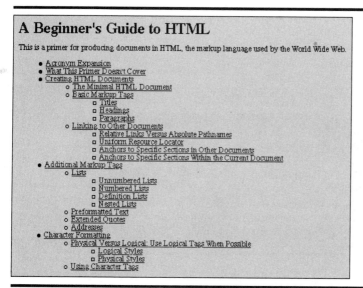

A Beginner's Guide to HTML

This is a primer for producing documents in HTML, the markup language used by the World Wide Web.

- Acronym Expansion
- What This Primer Doesn't Cover
- Creating HTML Documents
  - The Minimal HTML Document
  - Basic Markup Tags
    - Titles
    - Headings
    - Paragraphs
  - Linking to Other Documents
    - Relative Links Versus Absolute Pathnames
    - Uniform Resource Locator
    - Anchors to Specific Sections in Other Documents
    - Anchors to Specific Sections Within the Current Document
- Additional Markup Tags
  - Lists
    - Unnumbered Lists
    - Numbered Lists
    - Definition Lists
    - Nested Lists
  - Preformatted Text
  - Extended Quotes
  - Addresses
- Character Formatting
  - Physical Versus Logical: Use Logical Tags When Possible
    - Logical Styles
    - Physical Styles
  - Using Character Tags

Figure 2.83:
Writing your own home page becomes easier with sites such as the Beginner's Guide to HTML.

A Comprehensive Guide to Publishing on the Web

http://www.gnn.com/gnn/wic/html.05.html

Housed at the same site as the previous entry, the information you get here will help you actually get what you've created out there for people to see. Here you'll find some HTML information, along with guidelines for creating a site on the Web, how to publish your Web pages with WebCom, how to publicize your site, FAQs, and an icon index. This last section has links to indexes of icons and graphics, to sites with good icon/graphics collections, to graphics for HTML pages, to background images, and to free art to put in your own HTML pages.

Background Collection

http://weber.u.washington.edu/~pfloyd/backgrounds/backgrounds.html

At this site (which you can also get to through a link from the Comprehensive Guide to Publishing on the Web), you'll find 110 backgrounds for your home page, developed for your use by Jerry Russell. He'll also give you hints about finding good color schemes so that your text will be highly readable. (See Figure 2.84 for some possibilities; also see *Cloud Gallery* earlier in this book for other background ideas.)

Figure 2.84:
Individualize your
home page with public
domain backgrounds
from the Background
Collection.

Cut and Paste HTML

http://www.gnn.com/gnn/wic/html.13.html

One of the simplest ways to develop a home page (especially for the first time) is to take one you like, convert it to HTML, and change it as you see fit. It's a lot easier than creating one from scratch, and it's a nice place for beginners to start. At this site, you'll have the opportunity to learn how to do this most effectively. You'll get instructions on how to cut and paste HTML and how to set up a new document, headers, text styles, fonts, paragraphs and breaks, lines, links and anchors, lists, tables, and images, along with background about HTML and references.

Web66 Eight Minute HTML Primer

http://web66.coled.umn.edu/Cookbook/HTML/MinutePrimer.html

At this site, you'll be focused on eight aspects of HTML. It's suggested that you print out two copies of your page—the one written in HTML and the one that is the result of your programming. In that way, you can compare them and see if you'd like to do anything differently. The eight topics are TITLE, H#, B, I, P, HR, IMG, and A. When you know how to use these commands, you can get any Web page started. (See Figure 2.85 for a view of this page.)

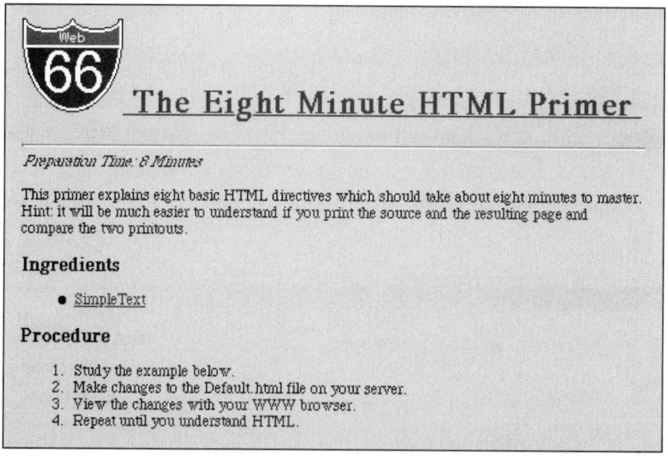

The Eight Minute HTML Primer

Figure 2.85:
Web66 offers eight-
minute tutorials for
HTML programming.

Preparation Time: 8 Minutes

This primer explains eight basic HTML directives which should take about eight minutes to master.
Hint: it will be much easier to understand if you print the source and the resulting page and
compare the two printouts.

Ingredients

- SimpleText

Procedure

1. Study the example below.
2. Make changes to the Default.html file on your server.
3. View the changes with your WWW browser.
4. Repeat until you understand HTML.

Carlos's FORMS Tutorial

http://robot0.ge.uiuc.edu/~carlosp/cs317/cft.html

This site gets you into forms immediately when you sign on. You'll be asked
your name and favorite color, which you select from a pull-down menu. This
information is then used to take you through creating forms of your own—a
nice addition to your home page.

American Indian Young People's Pages

http://niikaan.fdl.cc.mn.us/~isk/kidpage.html

At this site, kids and teachers learn to create Web pages. You'll find tips, tricks,
and traps in a tutorial, as well as How2 learn your own HTML methods,
including software and hardware tools.

The Web Developer's Virtual Library

http://www.charm.net/~web/Dr.Web/

At this site, you'll be able to find out about lots of aspects of HTML programming and home-page development. You can find out how to make alternate
bullets and scan images, find free Web space, get copyright information, find

sites for backdrops and pictures, and learn how to add today's date in HTML
code to your document. You'll also find Ask Dr. Web, where you can post a
message. You can ask a question, answer a question, or participate in a discussion. You'll be asked for your name and e-mail address and the subject of
your posting. You can link to your own page if you like. You're advised to take
a look at what's already been asked and answered before you jump in. Perhaps
your question has already been covered extensively, and you'll get your answer
immediately. (See Figure 2.86.)

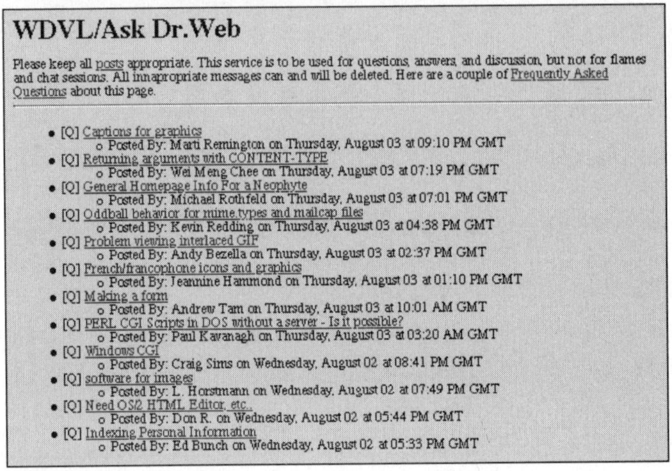

WDVL/Ask Dr.Web

Please keep all posts appropriate. This service is to be used for questions, answers, and discussion, but not for flames
and chat sessions. All innapropriate messages can and will be deleted. Here are a couple of Frequently Asked
Questions about this page.

- [Q] Captions for graphics
  - Posted By: Marti Remington on Thursday, August 03 at 09:10 PM GMT
- [Q] Returning arguments with CONTENT-TYPE
  - Posted By: Wei Meng Chee on Thursday, August 03 at 07:19 PM GMT
- [Q] General Homepage Info For a Neophyte
  - Posted By: Michael Rothfeld on Thursday, August 03 at 07:01 PM GMT
- [Q] Oddball behavior for mime types and mailcap files
  - Posted By: Kevin Redding on Thursday, August 03 at 04:38 PM GMT
- [Q] Problem viewing interlaced GIF
  - Posted By: Andy Bezella on Thursday, August 03 at 02:37 PM GMT
- [Q] French/francophone icons and graphics
  - Posted By: Jeannine Hammond on Thursday, August 03 at 01:10 PM GMT
- [Q] Making a form
  - Posted By: Andrew Tam on Thursday, August 03 at 10:01 AM GMT
- [Q] PERL CGI Scripts in DOS without a server - Is it possible?
  - Posted By: Paul Kavanagh on Thursday, August 03 at 03:20 AM GMT
- [Q] Windows CGI
  - Posted By: Craig Sims on Wednesday, August 02 at 08:41 PM GMT
- [Q] software for images
  - Posted By: L. Horstmann on Wednesday, August 02 at 07:49 PM GMT
- [Q] Need OS2 HTML Editor, etc.
  - Posted By: Don R. on Wednesday, August 02 at 05:44 PM GMT
- [Q] Indexing Personal Information
  - Posted By: Ed Bunch on Wednesday, August 02 at 05:33 PM GMT

Figure 2.86:
Most likely, Dr. Web
will have an answer to
your HTML program-
ming questions.

Appendices

A: Where Do I Go from Here?

B: Internet Service Providers

Where Do I Go from Here?

Now that you know the basics and what's out there on the Internet, you may want to find out more about using the Internet. For example, you may want to learn in more detail about the World Wide Web, Telnet, Gopher, and FTP, and about the software and tools you can use to make the most of your Internet travels. You'll be able to get information about your favorite band, travel to Hawaii to study volcanoes, contribute your poetry to online sites, or follow Monarch butterflies as they migrate.

If you'd like a basic, plain English tour of the Internet and its uses, *Easy Guide to the Internet,* by Christian Crumlish, is for you. It's like having an Internet guru at your side, explaining everything as you go along. Another great book for newbies is *Access the Internet,* by David Peal. This book even includes NetCruiser software, which will get you connected via an easy point-and-click interface in no time if you're using a DOS machine.

For an introduction to the World Wide Web, turn to *Surfing the Internet with Netscape* or *Mosaic Access to the Internet*, both by Daniel A. Tauber and Brenda Kienan. Each of these books walks you through getting connected, and they both include the Windows-based software you need to get started on the Web in a jiffy.

For quick and easy Internet reference, take a look at the *Internet Instant Reference,* by Paul Hoffman, and for an in-depth overview, try the best-selling *Internet Roadmap,* by Bennett Falk. To get familiar with the lingo, you can turn to the compact and concise *Internet Dictionary,* by Christian Crumlish.

If you've just got to learn all there is to know about the Internet, the comprehensive *Mastering the Internet,* by Glee Harrah Cady and Pat McGregor, is for you. And if you want to find out what tools and utilities are available (often on the Internet itself) to maximize the power of your Internet experience, you'll want to check out *The Internet Tool Kit,* by Nancy Cedeño.

All these books have been published by Sybex.

Internet Service Providers

If you need to set up an account with an Internet service provider, this is the place for you. This appendix lists providers in the United States, Canada, Great Britain, Ireland, Australia, and New Zealand.

The service providers listed here offer full Internet service, including SLIP/PPP accounts, which allow you to use Web browsers such as Mosaic and Netscape.

This list is by no means comprehensive. It concentrates on service providers that offer national or nearly national Internet service in English-speaking countries. You may prefer to go with a service provider that's local to your area—to minimize your phone bill, it is important to find a service provider that you can access via a local or toll-free phone number.

When you inquire into establishing an account with any of the providers listed in this appendix, tell them the type of account you want—you may want a shell account, if you know and plan to use Unix commands to get around, or you may want the type of point-and-click access that's offered through Netcom's NetCruiser. If you want to run a Web browser such as Mosaic or Netscape, you must have a SLIP or PPP account. Selecting an Internet service provider is a matter of personal preference and local access. Shop around, and if you aren't satisfied at any point, change providers.

What's Out There

Three very good sources of information about Internet service providers are available on the Internet itself. Peter Kaminski's Public Dialup Internet Access list (PDIAL) is at ftp.netcom.com/pub/in/info-deli/public-access/pdial.

Yahoo's Internet Access Providers list is at http://www.yahoo.com/Business/Corporations/Internet_Access_providers/.

CyberSpace Today's list is at http://www.cybertoday.com/.

IN THE UNITED STATES

In this section we list Internet service providers that offer local access phone numbers in most major American cities. These are the big, national companies. Many areas also have smaller regional Internet providers, which may offer better local access if you're not in a big city. You can find out about these smaller companies by looking in local computer papers such as *MicroTimes* or *Computer Currents* or by getting on the Internet via one of these big companies and checking out the Peter Kaminski, Yahoo, and CyberSpace Today service provider listings.

Netcom Netcom Online Communications Services is a national Internet service provider with local access numbers in most major cities. As of this writing, it has more than 100 local access numbers in the United States and an 800 access number for those who don't live near the local access numbers. Using the 800 number involves an additional fee. Netcom's NetCruiser software gives you point-and-click access to the Internet. (Netcom also provides a shell account, but stay away from it if you want to run Netscape.) Starting with NetCruiser version 1.6, it is possible to run Netscape on top of NetCruiser. Especially for beginning users who want a point-and-click interface and easy setup of Netscape, this may be a good choice

NetCruiser software is available on disk for free but without documentation at many trade shows and bookstores. It is also available with a very good book, *Access the Internet, Second Edition* (David Peal, Sybex, 1995), that shows you how to use the software. To contact Netcom directly, phone (800) 353-6600 or fax (408) 241-9145.

Performance Systems International (PSINet) Performance Systems International is a national Internet service provider with local access numbers in many American cities and in Japan. These folks are currently upgrading their modems to 28.8Kbps, which will give you faster access to the Internet.

To contact PSI directly, phone (800) 82P-SI82 or fax (800) FAXPSI-1.

UUNet/AlterNet UUNet Technologies and AlterNet offer Internet service throughout the United States. They run their own national network.

You can contact UUnet and AlterNet by phone at (800) 488-6383 or by fax at (703) 206-5601.

Portal Portal Communications, Inc., an Internet service provider in the San Francisco Bay Area, lets you get connected either by dialing one of its San Francisco Bay Area phone numbers or via the CompuServe network. (This is not CompuServe Information Services, but rather the network on which CompuServe runs.) The CompuServe network, with more than 400 access phone numbers, is a local call from most of the United States.

You can contact Portal by phone at (408) 973-9111 or by fax at (408) 752-1580.

IN CANADA

Listed here are providers that offer access to Internet service in the areas around large Canadian cities. For information about local access in less-populated regions, get connected and check out the Peter Kaminski, Yahoo, and CyberSpace Today lists described earlier in this appendix.

Many Internet service providers in the U.S. also offer service in Canada and in border towns near Canada. If you're interested and you're in Canada, you can ask some of the big U.S. service providers whether they have a local number near you.

UUNet Canada UUNet Canada is the Canadian division of the United States service provider UUNet/AlterNet, which we described earlier in this appendix. UUNet Canada offers Internet service to large portions of Canada.

You can contact UUNet Canada directly by phone at (416) 368-6621 or by fax at (416) 368-1350.

Internet Direct Internet Direct offers access to folks in the Toronto and Vancouver areas.

You can contact Internet Direct by phone at (604) 691-1600 or by fax at (604) 691-1605.

IN GREAT BRITAIN AND IRELAND

The Internet is, after all, international. Here are some service providers located and offering service in Great Britain and Ireland.

UNet Located in the northwest part of England, with more locations promised, UNet offers access at speeds up to 28.8K, along with various Internet tools for your use.

UNet can be reached by phone at 0925 633 144.

Easynet London-based Easynet provides Internet service throughout England via Pipex, along with a host of Internet tools.

You can reach Easynet by phone at 0171 209 0990.

Ireland On-Line Serving most (if not all) of Ireland, including Belfast, Ireland On-Line offers complete Internet service, including ISDN and leased-line connections.

Contact Ireland On-Line by phone at 00 353 (0)1 8551740.

IN AUSTRALIA AND NEW ZEALAND

Down under in Australia and New Zealand, the Internet is as popular as it is in the northern hemisphere; many terrific sites are located in Australia especially. Here are a couple of service providers for that part of the world.

Connect.com.au In wild and woolly Australia, Internet service (SLIP/PPP) is available from Connect.com.au Pty Ltd.

You can contact the people at Connect.com.au by phone at 61 3 528 2239.

Actrix Actrix Information Exchange offers Internet service (PPP accounts) in the Wellington, New Zealand area.

You can reach these folks by phone at 64 4 389 6316.

Index

Note to the Reader: Throughout this index **boldface** page numbers indicate primary discussions of a topic. *Italicized* page numbers indicate illustrations.